Winzig, Germany, 1933–1946

The seal of Winzig, Silesia, which was founded as a German town in 1285.

WINZIG, GERMANY, 1933–1946

The History of a Town under the Third Reich

RITA S. BOTWINICK

Westport, Connecticut
London

Library of Congress Cataloging-in-Publication Data

Botwinick, Rita S.
    Winzig, Germany, 1933-1946 : the history of a town under the Third
Reich / Rita S. Botwinick.
        p.   cm.
    Includes bibliographical references and index.
    ISBN 0-275-94185-X (alk. paper)
    1. Winzig (Germany)—History.   2. National socialism—Germany—
Winzig.   I. Title.
    DD801.W5844B68   1992
    943.1'5—dc20   91-35255

British Library Cataloguing in Publication Data is available.

Library of Congress Catalog Card Number: 91-35255
ISBN: 0-275-94185-X

First published in 1992

Praeger Publishers, 88 Post Road West, Westport, CT 06881
An imprint of Greenwood Publishing Group, Inc.

Printed in the United States of America

The paper used in this book complies with the
Permanent Paper Standard issued by the National
Information Standards Organization (Z39.48-1984).

10 9 8 7 6 5 4 3 2 1

Remembering Mikey,
a brief candle, but, oh, such light, such warmth.

Contents

Maps   ix

Introduction   1

1. The Good Old Days   9

2. Victory by Default   23

3. Something Ventured, Nothing Gained   39

4. Anti-Semitism: Blight and Flight   61

5. The Death of Winzig   87

6. The Oder-Neisse Line: Focus of Conflicting
   Claims   111

Notes   135

Annotated Bibliography   141

Index   147

Photographs   following page 60

Maps

Silesia in 1939   8

Winzig in 1939   22

Poland, Territorial Changes in 1939-1945   86

Central Europe in 1990   132

NOTE: All chronicles, letters, and historical accounts that were written in German were translated by the author.

Introduction

Winzig, Germany, 1933-1946, is an account of events that occurred in an obscure little German town located in southeastern Prussia in a region that for hundreds of years has been known as Silesia. In the geographic sense, the town survived. A Polish village called Winsco is located on that same hill east of the Odra (Oder) River in western Poland where Winzig had stood for half a millennium. Some of the old buildings still remain; very little has been added in the past forty-five years. But if a town's life is judged by the character of its inhabitants, Winzig no longer exists. Its ancient German roots have been pulled up. This is the chronicle of how that happened.

Allowing for the uniqueness of every community, Winzig presents a microcosm of the convulsive Nazi era. Only in the memories of those who lost their homes was Winzig ever an idyllic place. Its people were quite typical of those living in most small towns: gossipy, petty, class conscious, conservative, patriotic, and hardworking. When Hitler came to power, Winzig produced its quota of heroes, villains, and bystanders.

Even a town as small as Winzig cannot be abstracted in all its facets. This record utilizes several families as representatives of the community: Nazis and anti-Nazis; Jews and Gentiles; Catholics and Protestants; farmers, merchants, and professionals. It is a portrait that includes a glimpse of a gamut of personalities: the blindly devout followers of Nazi ideology, the opportunists seeking economic advancement, the few active opponents to the regime, as well a sampling from the largest group, the silent, fearful people who sought safety as nonpolitical spectators.

A word of explanation seems in order concerning the selection of Winzig as the topic of this research. Why not a large city such as Breslau or Stettin? The answer lies in the personal relationship of the author to the town. I was born and grew up in Winzig. Despite the interruption of the war, old contacts and friendships were never severed, and thus it was possible to collect material and conduct interviews with the actual participants in the events. In an atmosphere of familiarity, not only words but often emotions were shared.

But why do we need yet another book on the Nazi era? Library shelves are already overflowing with the records of Germany's experiment with national madness. What purpose is served by an examination of such an insignificant, commonplace little German market town? No one important ever lived there, nothing remarkable was ever achieved there. Its people were ordinary-the bearers, not the makers, of human destiny. To the writer and reader of history the inhabitants of a town like Winzig are usually nameless, faceless statistics. They are part of the masses who never touch us, whose lives and deaths are represented by numbers. The time has come, indeed it is long due, to see the shapes and distinguish the faces of individuals with all their remarkable differences. Historical records, so rich in dissertations of the great and famous, rarely portray the Nazi years from the worm's-eye view of the ordinary folk. The tendency to regard the German people as a monolithic mass, hypnotized by Hitler into a state of delusion, has blurred the great variety of responses among the German people to the tensions of the Nazi years.

Germany had experienced continuous social, economic, and political upheaval since the First World War. The rate and depth of further change was greatly accelerated during the Nazi era. How did families cope with the impermanence of their world? Accounts of individual Winzigers affirm the important role of fear in propelling behavior. But fear does not create uniformity. Reactions to oppression ran the full gamut from courage to cowardice, from defiance to compliance.

Ambition, or greed masquerading as ambition, was alive and well in Winzig. The Nazi regime offered the traditional underclass of the landless rare opportunities for advancement. Now the envy of the have-nots could be translated into activity; the bottom layer of society could elbow out their betters as qualifications for a variety of employment opportunities were pegged to Nazi party membership. To wear the swastika required no education, no experience, and the benefits were immediate. The microcosm of Winzig cannot answer the riddle of why some people would not, or could not, be divorced from their basic decency and humanity no matter what the cost. Winzig's fine example, Rektor Spieler, was well educated, but not uniquely so; he attended Protestant religious services often, but not always. His upbringing was mirrored in thousands of Silesian homes. What made him a righteous man? When asked why he was willing to risk so much in his struggle against the local Nazi power structure, he replied, "There was nothing else I could do."

It is tempting to generalize the events in Winzig and apply them to a larger design; so that is how the Nazis came to power in rural Germany; so that is how the people reacted; so that is what happened during the Soviet invasion; so that is how the Poles took control of the eastern region. In many instances such a universalization is valid, but there is neither pledge nor promise that such translation from the specific to the general will always apply.

And yet the story of Winzig is not a singular episode in German life. Here, as in most German towns, the worst element acquired political leadership. Anti-Nazi political parties succumbed with but a whimper. Even the unsuccessful attempt to bring a more respectable group to power locally was echoed in other towns. Many Winzigers welcomed the early economic improvement promoted by the Nazi regime, as did most Germans. And the voice of Hugo Kliem was the voice of millions when he said, "That upstart, that nobody, that Hitler, he's making things work. If only he didn't . . ."

Winzig's reactions to the rise of Hitler, to the twelve years of Nazi tyranny, to the collapse of the nation at the close of the war, and, finally, to the expulsion of the population from the eastern third of the country were-in fact, are-phenomena that are unique as well as universal. Precisely because its residents were so conventional in their decency and indecency, their blindness and awareness, their courage and self-seeking, they mirror the German condition, even though such reflections never reproduce with perfect fidelity.

The people of Winzig shared a common fate with some 10 million Germans who lived east of the Oder-Neisse Line before 1946. The scenes of the closing months of the Nazi regime were, in their essence, a collective drama. Geography determined that Winzigers suffered an early invasion by Soviet armies, and geography ordained their expulsion when this area was ceded to Poland. The same geography exacted its price from the entire region as new boundaries were drawn by Soviet politicians. The people involved in the consequent upheaval were powerless, even voiceless. One of the cruelest decisions of Goebbels's Propaganda Ministry was to forbid German municipalities the right to take specific individual action in the face of the Soviet breakthrough. Only the *Gauleiters*, the provincial heads of the Nazi party, could issue orders of evacuation. These *Gauleiters* were political hacks trying to prove their loyalty to the disintegrating regime by refusing to admit that German troops could not delay the Soviet advance. The result of this callousness was unnecessary chaos and loss of civilian lives.

Internal events in prewar Nazi Winzig were imprecisely mirrored elsewhere in Germany. Towns all over the country experienced intraparty struggles for leadership. Winzig's trial of a Nazi faithful by a party court, though uncommon, was not a singular occurrence, and the dismissal of an anti-Nazi such as Rektor Spieler was not at all extraordinary. Attempts to retain old and cherished values met the same fate everywhere. There simply was no chance for their public survival.

The people of Winzig were neither ciphers nor goose-stepping, machine-cast robots. Though their ability to make choices was, by U.S. standards, severely limited, individuals could and often did exercise their will. The notion, dear to revisionists, that all of Germany was one huge concentration camp cannot be supported by the evidence. The convenience of painting Hitler's German society with a broad brush must be abandoned.

Winzig had several Jewish families. Their ordeal also conformed to the general theme of universality and uniqueness.

Although Jewish farmers like the Steinhardts were uncommon and the resourcefulness of the head of the family was remarkable, many aspects of the destiny of this little group were shared by hundreds of thousands of German Jews. Typically, the reactions of old friends and neighbors ranged from overt malevolence to covert *Schadenfreude* (joy in someone else's misfortune) and from careless indifference to careful distancing. Rarely did the Jews experience open support but, occasionally secret help was extended. Before the implementation of the Final Solution, these were the prevailing experiences of most German Jews.

The fate of Winzig was the fate of the eastern provinces during the final months of the war. The Soviet invasion and occupation was followed by the Polish domination, which was followed in turn by the expulsion of the native German population. Because of the abhorrent nature of Nazi inhumanity and of the Holocaust in particular, there has been general silence on the suffering of the German civilian population. Military actions, such as the bombing of Dresden, were accepted as necessary wartime measures. Of the fate of Germans east of the Oder-Neisse Line little is known. It is the function of the recorder of history to set down what happened with as little bias as is humanly possible. The removal of 10 million civilians from their homeland is a fact of historical significance that deserves a place in the annals of this century.

The account of the people of Winzig who were expelled from their homes was reenacted with some local differences in all the territories the U.S.S.R. awarded to Poland. Events sorted themselves into a sequence of three acts.

First, the cowardice of the Nazi *Gauleiters* prevented an orderly evacuation before the onslaught of the Soviet armies crossing into Reich territories. The flight of the civilian population was generally disorganized and, no doubt, needlessly agonizing.

Second, the Soviet army behaved no worse nor better than the Germans should have expected, particularly in view of the atrocities committed by the German occupiers of the Soviet Union.

Third, the Politburo of the U.S.S.R. kept its own agenda and unilaterally ceded the territory east of the Oder-Neisse Line to its Polish satellite. The Polish occupation forces ordered the expulsion of the native population with the consent of their Big Brother. The U.S.S.R. had occupied Polish lands on her own western frontier, and the German provinces served to compensate Poland for these losses. The fate of Winzig between 1945 and 1946 was experienced by hundreds of villages, many towns, and several large cities when Soviet troops invaded and when the German-Polish border was shifted. Three volumes of depositions gathered by the West German government (*Dokumentation der Vertreibung der Deutschen aus Ost- Mitteleuropa: Die Vertreibung der deutschen Bevoelkerung aus den Gebieten Oestlich der Oder-Neisse*) record the trauma. The accounts given by the victims are variations of similar themes of suffering, confusion, and anger experienced by the refugees from Winzig. They were betrayed. In fact, betrayed twice. Their own leaders lied to them about the certainty of German victory, and then the Western Allies, by their acquiescence to the demands of the Soviet Union, condemned them to exile.

There is another dimension to the history of Winzig, namely, the inquiry into the fate of the expelled population. Where did they go? Did they languish in camps set up by the United Nations? Were they rejected by their fellow Germans? What acts of violence and terrorism have been committed by the expatriates to regain their lost homeland? Who has given them financial support? Have they received compensation for their property losses?

The answers are not found in the headlines of the international press. A quiet triumph, as remarkable as the much vaunted economic recovery of Germany, was effected by the people and governments of postwar Germany. When the Oder-Neisse Line became the new German boundary and native population was forced to leave, a destitute, devastated, morally outcast Germany faced the burden of millions of generally penniless arrivals from the east. Yet the process was a remarkable success. The goodwill of most of the indigenous population who accommodated the newcomers, the hard work of the arrivals, and some aid from the authorities combined to make the integration of 10 million people a historic reality. In fact, the process was so unobtrusive, it has remained a no-news item, undeserving of public attention. Amazing? Indeed! Most of the Winzigers and their fellow exiles who made the trek to the west in 1946 are no longer alive. Their children and grandchildren cannot share their longing or their memories of the old homeland. They live in the present tense as part of the mainstream of German life. The relocation of millions of impoverished Germans from lands that their forefathers had held for many hundreds of years was accomplished without fanfare or warfare. That too is a part of the story of Winzig.

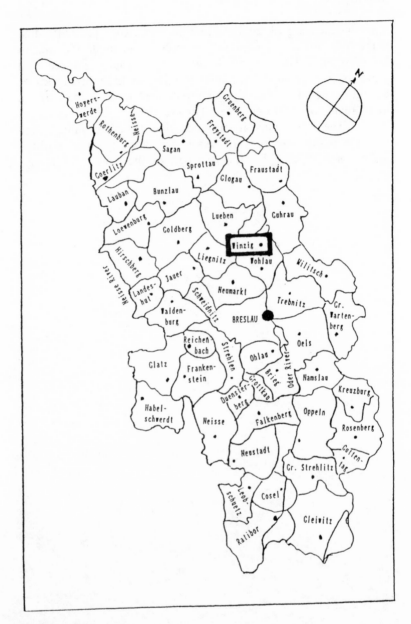

Silesia in 1939

1

The Good Old Days

A traveler approaching Winzig from any direction was greeted by a pleasant view; on a gently rounded hill, overlooking the countryside for miles around, nestled a compact, orderly little town. The name of the town, Winzig, which means "tiny" in German, might evoke a smile: a tiny community called Tiny. Actually, the derivation of the name stemmed from Winzer, grower of the grapes that once flourished on those green slopes. The town's coat of arms bore witness to the past; a rather stern-looking knight in armor holding an oversized sword in one hand and a fruited grapevine in the other. Protection for the land and its bounty is, indeed, an ancient concern of mankind.

Though unspectacular, the town had a comfortable look. Several hundred brick or stone buildings were arranged along tree lined streets with an air of timelessness and order. The slim gothic spire of the Protestant church, a landmark visible for thirty miles, dominated the horizon, while the Catholic church with its own bell tower maintained a proper and respectful secondary position. This, after all, was central Silesia, where Prussianism and Protestantism affirmed their centuries-old partnership. Winzig was encircled by an intricate patchwork of fields. On the best plots crops such as barley, oats, and rye were cultivated, and where the clay content colored the earth a shiny ocher, potatoes and sugar beets did well. Forests and meadows added their own hues of bright and dark greens, and in spring and summer this world was alive with wildflowers and the sounds of birds and insects. Stones, the curse of Silesian farmers, were heaped in piles along the boundaries separating fields. No matter how diligently the backbreaking job of rock clearing had been done, each plowing brought up a new crop. Where nothing else would thrive, goats, able to feed on coarse grasses and underbrush, augmented the marginal farmers' meat and milk supply. Every acre was utilized, valued not only as a livelihood but also as a sacrosanct family heritage.

Winzig was located in the state of Prussia, the province of Silesia, the administrative district of Breslau, and the county of Wohlau. Many of its residents had lived there, some in the very same houses, for hundreds of years. Winzigers identified themselves proudly as Silesians rather than Prussians. Their dialect, with its rolling r's, was quite distinct. Western Germans immediately recognized and often disparaged the Silesian vernacular. Not only was this a language rich in local idioms, but even its pattern of speech varied from High German. Such differences promoted a sense of solidarity and pride among the rural population while the urban Silesians seemed anxious to adapt their speech to that of the German mainstream.

Since prehistoric times Silesia had been a crossroad for various Slavic and Teutonic tribes moving west and east, always diversifying the cultural and genetic makeup of its people. Archaeological evidence identifies the Illyrians as Silesia's earliest inhabitants. About 300 B.C.E. the Celts traversed the area on their way to the Ukraine. Germanic tribes including the Vandals occupied the territory for some five hundred years, and the name Silesia was probably derived from a branch of the Vandals, the Sillingi. Slavic settlers filtered in during the sixth and seventh centuries C.E. and the Piast dynasty of Poland established its suzerainty after 1100.[1]

The holy Hedwig, patron saint of the region, exemplifies the mixed heritage of the land. She was the Bavarian born wife of Henry I, greatest of the Piast rulers. The late Middle Ages witnessed Bohemian and Austrian dominion, and in 1742 the territory passed into the Prussian hands of Fredrick the Great. Since then Silesia was part of Prussia, and after unification in 1871, was incorporated into the German nation.[2] In 1946 Silesia was appropriated by Poland.

By U.S. standards Winzig's roots were ancient. Its first charter was granted in 1285. Venerable? Yes, but not exceptional! Many European communities are able to trace a thousand years of continuity. Perhaps even more noteworthy is the fact that according to existing chronicles, nothing particularly remarkable or terrible ever happened there in nearly seven hundred years. The town remained small; it could claim no famous sons or daughters, no great battles, not even a castle to give it a touch of class. The great expectations that the construction of a railway spur would breathe new life into the town's ancient bones were never realized. In fact, the unification of the Reich, which brought industrial and commercial expansion to many areas, left Winzig basically untouched.[3]

The more prosperous neighboring towns of Wohlau and Steinau assumed an irritatingly paternalistic attitude toward Winzig. Wohlau, twenty kilometers to the south and the county seat, thrived as administrative bureaus multiplied. Steinau, fifteen kilometers southwest, was on the Oder River, and its historic markers commemorated the battles fought there for centuries by Poles, Bohemians, Mongols, Austrians, Hungarians, and Prussians. Thus the river and its defense bestowed upon Steinau an importance Winzig could not rival.

The primary cause of Winzig's stagnation was the lack of a reliable water source. Because most of the wells dried up during the summers no industry could flourish there.

Even in the twentieth century, Winzig displayed the flaws and flavors of medieval town planning. Though the encircling walls had disappeared long ago, their effects persisted: high, narrow-fronted houses in the center and sprawling farms around the perimeter of the town. Quite typically, the inner core of Winzig was called the Ring, but inappropriately, because it was a quadrangle. Here the city hall stood, stone gray and somber, overlooking the four main arteries that fed a continual trickle of traffic into the center. The clattering noise of horse drawn wagons on the round paving stones had remained unaltered for centuries. An automobile was a rarity until the mid-1930s. The Ring was Winzig's best commercial address. It was the hub of business for the pharmacy, several clothing stores, one of the two doctors, the printer who published a weekly newspaper, two lawyers, several dry goods merchants, the bank, and even a taxidermist with a molting owl in the window. The Schwarze Adler, a handsome building that combined the functions of a hotel, restaurant, and bar, and a small distillery and wine shop were among the establishments that provided for a little gemuetlichkeit. Most of the shops were located on the ground floor, with living quarters above.

Away from the center of town were the trades so vital to an agrarian community. Spread out along tree-lined roads were the workshops and dwellings of several blacksmiths, a wheel-right, two or three carpenters, two grain millers, and some seed, fertilizer, and cattle dealers. Dr. Schote, the veterinarian, whose skill could give or take the bread from a farmer's table, owned a lovely villa set in a splendid garden. Rektor Spieler, the school's principal, had built a picture postcard home, flowers in front, vegetable garden in back, and white sand on the boxwood-lined paths.

The areas between the open countryside and the Ring were held by Winzig's farmers. Their homes faced the street with an appearance of neatness, but usually the yards were cluttered with machinery, rusted and new, some usable and others dilapidated, and an assortment of sheds of all kinds. Poultry and pigs competed for rights to the inevitable dung heap. Often the barn was in better condition than the house and the livestock better nourished than the family. Unlike their U.S. counterparts, European farmers did not (and still do not) build homes on their fields but traditionally sought refuge behind the walls of towns or feudal castles. This arrangement, reasonable in the age of medieval warfare, persisted into the atomic age. Sons lived in the homes inherited from their fathers, generation after generation. The distribution of landholdings, too, was a holdover from the past. No grand expanse of swaying grain or boundless forests here, but narrow ribbons of fields, etched by stone fences or ridges of untended grass. Not one of the town's farmers held land in a single plot; some worked as many as ten strips, separated by the properties of a score of other owners. Any suggestion to change this impractical arrangement by buying, selling, or trading was regarded as somewhere between absurd and heretical.

Farmers comprised the majority of the inhabitants of Winzig. They were generally conservative, willing to let the past dictate the present and the future. Their attachment to those inherited plots of land, whether sizable or five acres, was the fixed foundation of their lives. For the sake of their fields, which were often forever stony, swampy, or sandy, no sacrifice was too dear.

Some of Winzig's peasants lived in dire poverty. Their houses had earthen floors, water had to be carried from pumps in the street, perhaps for a considerable distance, and only one room, the kitchen, was heated in winter. Their children wore each other's shoes when the temperatures fell to freezing, and the mainstay of their diet was potatoes. Debt and the specter of bankruptcy lived within their walls, along with the mice under the floorboards and the flies that blackened the windows in summer. Nonetheless, they clung to their unrewarding, bone-wearying labor in a devotion to the soil that defied all reason.

The basis of the central Silesian economy was agriculture. Much of the land was in the hands of large estate owners, known as the *Rittergutsbesitzer*, frequently the descendants of lesser nobility. In the past their forebears may have been feudal lords who worked the land with serfs. Even into the twentieth century they often managed to retain the best parts of their former holdings, ranging from two hundred to five hundred acres. Nor had they ceased to be a formidable social and political force. The great-grandchildren of the former serfs frequently had remained on the estates, where they became hired laborers. Their arrangements with the landlord resembled those of American sharecroppers. Small homesteaders, whose acreage rarely exceeded one hundred, made up the majority of farmers in Winzig.[4] While they willingly accepted the social and economic prominence of the estate owners, they jealously guarded their own superior condition over their landless neighbors. This class stratification was ancient, continual, and uncompromising.

The suicide of Ernst Kliem in 1932 serves as a case in point. Ernst was the oldest son of a respected, long-established family, five hundred years on the same land. Ernst had the misfortune to fall in love with the daughter of a mere day laborer. He was in his early twenties; the beautiful, impoverished girl was in her teens. Kliem senior forbade his son to continue the relationship and expected the usual immediate and automatic obedience from his son. But Ernst's love was stronger then his filial duty. He quarreled violently with his father. Frau Kliem was no help. She stood aside silently. Threats of disinheritance flew through the air and were countered with escalating defiance. Finally the father presented Ernst with an ultimatum: choose between the farm and the girl. But the young man could part with neither; he solved the dilemma by hanging himself from a rafter in the barn.

The tragedy was discussed endlessly in the shops, across the fences, and around the water pumps, but while tears were shed for Ernst and his unhappy love, no criticism was leveled against the father. His action had been in keeping with the local code of proper parental behavior.

The past dominated Winzig even in the structure of its houses. Visitors from the Rhineland often wondered why Silesian buildings bore such a striking resemblance to their own architectural style. These similarities were not coincidental. They were the consequence of a call for Rhinish settlers issued by thirteenth-century Piast kings. The skills of the Rhine-laenders were welcomed in the Oder valley, and as the Frankish people established themselves they transplanted their architecture. A Polish dynasty thus tied Silesia culturally to the German west.

Winzig's homes were not built for comfort; they were planted in the ground to provide shelter. Thick walls were constructed of stone or brick, with some wooden gables set into the stuccoed second story. Ventilation, was not important, screens were unheard of and windows were small and almost always closed. Only a few of the farmhouses had indoor plumbing. Carrying endless pails of water from the pumps bent the backs of the women, often into permanent curvatures. Cooking was done on stoves constantly greedy for wood or coal. Wash day was a monthly affair that entailed boiling, scrubbing, rinsing, outdoor drying, mangling and ironing. During the harvest season, farmers' wives and daughters worked side by side with the men. At the poorer homesteads, women helped with milking and cared for the barnyard fowl as well. Household and child-rearing functions were subordinate to farm work. No wonder these women aged so rapidly, but on this level of society there was no weaker sex. If a landowner had a good year, the weather had been right, prices had held and his animals remained healthy, he plowed the profits back into the farm: a better barn, a new piece of machinery, a fine breeding bull. Possessions that merely enhanced one's comfort or gave pleasure were considered extravagances, and few transgressions were as repugnant as waste. Considering the austerity of life (were it not for the availability of electricity, primitiveness would have been an apt description), the phenomenon of the *gute Stube* was indeed curious. This was a sitting room where one rarely sat, a showplace for china plates, embroidered pillows, crocheted doilies, and formal family photographs. The best furniture in the house hid under old sheets and precious bits and pieces from generations of dowries collected dust. Any guest invited into the *gute Stube* knew that he had been granted a distinction. Only on special occasions, perhaps Christmas Eve or to celebrate a wedding, was the room aired to clear away the odor of mothballs. Despite its infrequent use, ownership of a *gute Stube* was important, a social necessity, perhaps a refuge from the shabbiness of daily life.

Approximately 85 percent of Winzig's population of 2,200 were members of the Evangelical church; some 15 percent was Catholic, and less then 1 percent was Jewish. Enrollment in the Catholic school was small due to the perception that the larger Protestant school offered a better education. Also, the *Volksschule* or public school offered the brightest students the opportunity to attend three upper-level classes; passing through Winzig's sexta, quinta, and quarta courses gave a small, select group of students the opportunity to transfer to a *Gymnasium* for a secondary education. Although the *Abitur*, roughly equivalent to an associate or two-year degree, was achieved by an estimated 5-10 percent (mostly the children of the well-to-do), completion of a university education by one of Winzig's own was rare enough to generate pride, envy, and mention on the front page of the local newspaper.

For most of the children, school was an affliction to be borne like the coughs in winter and beestings in summer. While the three R's, geography, history, literature, and sewing skills for girls and shop instruction for boys were taught with varying success, the school also functioned significantly in the process of taming the spirit of the young. As a colt had to be accustomed to the reins, so future taxpayers needed to be readied to accept their destiny of toil and obedience. The school building of gray stone and its bare cobblestoned yard stated irrefutably that learning was a serious pursuit. The educational system permitted little local autonomy. It was a centrally directed national function. The objective was clear: mold the young into a disciplined, literate, hardworking, patriotic citizenry. Orderliness was a virtue to be pursued with zeal. Neatness mattered a great deal, as did punctuality and respectfulness. Competition within the classroom was encouraged, but rarely the expression of critical thoughts or attitudes. While overt cruelty by the teachers was unacceptable, the enforcement of rules with the cane was commonplace; girls stood with palms up; boys leaned over a chair. Parents insisted that these school years were the happiest of all. Few children would have agreed. Their right to be young, silly, and carefree was stifled by an educational system that regarded laughter as a punishable offense.

Winzig's religious life was a bright thread running through the center of the fabric of town life. Sundays were the best days. Nearly all the women and children and some of the men put on their good clothes and leisurely made their way to either the Protestant or the Catholic church. On holidays every pew was occupied and the congregations took pride and pleasure in the singing of their respective choirs. A special dinner was served in the early afternoon, and the admonition that this be a day of rest was heeded as much as the necessary farm chores permitted.

On one of Winzig's side streets stood the one room synagogue. It sprang to life only during the High Holy Days, when an itinerant rabbi led the services. The handful of Jewish families could not support a permanent rabbi. Before 1933 the Jewish community celebrated its festivals undisturbed by either private or official hostility. Anti-Semitism existed, but on an impersonal level. It was directed toward a concept, not toward individual Jews. Somewhere, perhaps in the big cities, there were Jews who did not fit into German life, but "our" Jews were decent and hardworking.

The role of the churches created some barriers between Catholics and Protestants and obviously between Christians and Jews as well, but one cannot speak of aversion based on faith. Although Winzig's social life tended to pivot around religious activities, close friendships were formed that crossed church

affiliations. The bonds of class bridged scriptural differences.
Professionals invited one another into their homes. Important
farmers, merchants and artisans sought each other's company
without awkwardness. Jews and Christians alike connected
socially and amiably. This situation, of course, changed greatly
during the Nazi years.

Winzig was a peaceable place. During the twenties and
thirties it had one policeman: the overweight Wachmeister
Urban. He walked his rounds every day. In twenty years he
never drew his revolver and only rarely made an arrest. The
town jail consisted of a small room with a barred window
located in the basement of the city hall. Drunkenness was of no
public concern; theft was rare and robbery unknown. Parents
disciplined their own young offenders, usually more severely
than the town ordinances. Urban not only knew every resident
in town, but could identify their horses, a useful skill, since it
enabled him to determine whom he might join for a beer. Only
four times a year did the good *Wachmeister* actually work at
keeping the peace, and that was at the fair, the wonderful,
tumultuous, exciting *Jahrmarkt*. Except for the annual children's
festival, nothing equaled the fair in transforming staid and
imperturbable Winzig into a bubbling spectacle. Dozens of
booths and tents sprang up, apparently overnight. The gray
Ring blossomed with colorful merchandise, and the voices of
the hawkers filled the air with exaggerated promises. Most of
the items were trinkets, novelties, toys, gadgets, and sugary
confections that looked much better than they tasted. Nevertheless, the crowds came all day, to look, to be part of the noise,
perhaps to buy something frivolous. Children, clutching small
coins, were everywhere, since schools were dismissed early. A
dancing bear or the organ-grinder's monkey attracted wide-eyed
admirers, but nothing could challenge the popularity of the poor
man's minstrel, the *Baenkelsaenger*. He was dressed quite
formally, in black suit and tie, as he stood on his little bench,
his *Baenkel*, so all could see and hear him. Several screens
with brilliantly painted pictures were unrolled to his right and
his left, and as he sang he pointed to the appropriate illustration. His musical verses dealt with brave foresters, chaste
maidens, and lustful landowners. When he reached the critical
point where evil must surely triumph, he offered his listeners

a booklet for five pennies, a mere five pennies, to find out if the hero found a way to save the trembling, wide-eyed heroine. "Not to be read by children!" he warned as he stuffed the coins into his pockets.

A picture of Winzig without a sketch of the children's festival, the *Kinderfest*, would reproduce a landscape without using the brightest hues on the palette. Every year, starting in the early spring, the town entered into weeks of feverish activity, which culminated in the *Kinderfest*. Just before the summer recess closed the schools, the people of Winzig gave themselves a present: two days of festivities. The first day was given to the entertainment of adults, the second dedicated to the children. The year 1934 marked the centennial of the event, a very special occasion. Rektor Spieler of the *Volksschule* was in charge of the arrangements.

Every social and civic organization contributed and participated. Everyone for miles around attended. Although the population of Winzig numbered 2,200, over 3,000 took part in the celebration. The festivities began with a formal procession through the city streets, three miles along the Steinauerstrasse to the forest, the Lustwald. So many ribbons, such an array of flowers. The horses pulling the floats were festooned, and how glossy were their coats, how brilliantly black their polished hooves. The town's history was recalled by an armored knight amid the vines. A cavalry troop in splendid uniforms of Fredrick the Great vintage celebrated the annexation of Silesia to Prussia and recalled that a garrison had been stationed in Winzig until 1880. Every guild marched in the garb of its trade. The millers in starched white next to the chimney sweeps in coal black, butchers, bakers, even the grave diggers were represented. The gymnastic club previewed the precision of their later performance. Bicyclists had woven streamers through the spokes of their wheels so that each rotation produced a colorful kaleidoscope. The schoolchildren were led by their teachers. The previous year's queen of the *Kinderfest*, the girl who had won the athletic competitions, walked under a cornflower crown held above her head by her four ladies-in-waiting. The school band played with more heart than talent, and Wohlau, as a token of friendship, had sent its city orchestra to give additional oompah-pah to the proceedings. On to the Lustwald where the very trees stood in green splendor. Mixed and men's choirs competed in good-natured rivalry. A play was performed under the branches of an old oak. Sports clubs invited the participation of young and old. Of course, lots of good food and drink oiled the machinery of the merry-making. At nightfall the children lit their Japanese lanterns, and in that magical light the new queen was escorted home by her weary, happy followers.[5]

Winzig's political life was based on a *Kabinetsorder* of the Prussian king, Wilhelm I, which regulated the government of towns. In accordance with that law, the voters could elect a council (until 1918 the three-class system of voting was in effect; direct elections were instituted after World War I). The councilmen selected one of their own as mayor, also a deputy mayor and three department heads in charge of farm and forest, assistance to the poor and official transactions, respectively. The Department of Official Transactions handled the arrangements for the quarterly fair. Although the mayor was the chief executive, real power was in the hands of the chairman of the council, usually a prosperous farmer.[6]

Local politics followed economic lines: farmer versus tradesman, and so forth. During the Weimar Republic, the conservative umbrella organization known as the Stahlhelm had room for nearly all of Winzig's political opinions. This was true as well during the decades between the world wars when German socialists dominated the national scene and the Communist and German Worker's parties attracted great numbers of voters in the cities. Rural Silesia remained conservative. Rektor Spieler ranked Winzig's political composition as follows:

1. German-National People's party
2. German People's party
3. Center party
4. Social Democratic party
5. German Democratic party

The last two organizations drew a mere handful of votes. Had not the kaiser himself proclaimed the revolutionary doctrine of socialism as the faith of unpatriotic ne'er-do- wells?

The monarchy was defunct, but in agrarian areas it continued to claim the loyalty of the majority. The German-National People's party represented the interests of the landowners. The German People's party spoke for the business community. Most Catholics voted the Center party, and liberals divided their meager strength between the Social Democratic and German Democratic parties. Political issues lay dormant for months and years and moved to center stage only with the approach of elections.[7] To the people of Winzig, local politics were always more interesting than the machinations in Breslau and Berlin.

The substance and flavor of Winzig politics were illustrated by an event described by one of its chroniclers, Walter Wittmann: In 1902, upon the death of the old mayor, the council was casting about for a replacement. The administrative eagles from Breslau, the provincial capital, suggested that Winzig provide a cozy berth for someone from their oversupply of retired officers. This offer had been accepted in the past, and Winzig had no wish to be saddled again with one of those untamed stallions. So the council advertised publicly for a candidate. The choice fell upon a certain Krause; he came with a good reputation from another small Silesian town. He struck an impressive pose and twirled his mustache in the manner of Wilhelm II. Before the selection became official, Krause made the rounds, visited the important folk, and voiced opinions ranging from arch- to liberal conservatism, according to the views of his host. Thus, having satisfied one and all, Krause was chosen unanimously. He was a satisfactory mayor, a good member of the rifle club, loyal to his adopted town, and everyone said that Frau Krause's heart was in the right place. But gradually clouds gathered on his horizon, and the darkest was in the shape of the master baker, Schilk. According to Wittmann, the Schilks had expected to socialize with the mayor and in anticipation had purchased a fine new living room set. But the expensive sofa did not draw the Krauses, who were cavorting with the elite-the doctor, the lawyer, the pharmacist and some of the influential farmers. The plot began to thicken when the baker's oldest son sowed his wild oats a bit too wildly. The mischief became a police matter, and proud Schilk had to plead for his son with the mayor. The fact that Krause was sympathetic and that the charges were dropped did not ease the pain for the petitioner who had stood, hat in hand, before the man who had spurned his friendship.

The town was soon divided between the Schilk and Krause factions. The baker reported every slight administrative irregularity to the county supervisor in Wohlau. But although Krause was troubled and distressed, nothing was discovered that called for his dismissal. Suddenly, in 1919, a shot rang out that shook Winzig's social foundation, a shot through the head of the mayor inflicted by his own hand. The funeral turned into a mobilization of indignation against the master baker's group, which was held responsible for hounding an innocent man to death. Before all this bad blood could coagulate, the town experienced another shock. Several weeks after her husband's death, Frau Krause had neatly bundled up all her husband's papers and sent them to the county administrator's office. Among the memos were receipts for billeting the Fifty-first HomeGuard Regiment during World War I. The mayor had cashed the checks and deposited the money into his own pocket.[8]

Baker Schilk and his friends were vindicated. As a result, in the future political power would rest on a broader base. The coalition between the powerful farmers and their allies from the professions was broken as authority shifted to the petty bourgeoisie. The next mayor, Walter Aust, gave the town an outstanding administration that served the interests of the entire community. His removal from office during the early 1930s is covered in the examination into events in Winzig during the Nazi years.

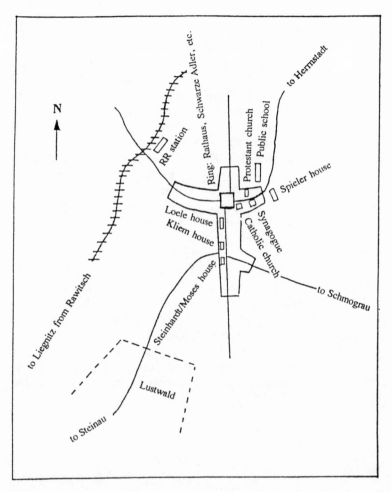

Winzig in 1939

2

Victory by Default

Conservative Winzig missed the monarchy. The deposed emperor Wilhelm II, was splitting wood in Holland while the nation staggered under the punishment inflicted by the provisions of the Treaty of Versailles. The Weimar Republic had been born amid great suffering, a lost war, hunger, and revolution. The democracy it proclaimed was but a tender shoot; only time and generations could assure its survival. It endured for a brief fifteen years, years too troubled and too few to allow the republic to take root. The decade of the twenties, with its unemployment, financial chaos, and violence in the streets, generated disillusionment and impatience punctuated by political assassinations. With each new disaster, the days of the monarchy took on ever-rosier hues for the conservatives. For others, the quick fixes offered by the radical right and the radical left held the promise of a better future. No groundswell of loyalty, no patriotic fervor, was able to germinate in support of the new democratic regime. The aristocracy sneered, the intellectuals debated, the middle class shrugged, the military fumed, and the working class cursed. Parliamentary government produced no charismatic leaders. It was unable to compete with either the romantic shadows of the past or the pie-in-the-sky rhetoric of the politicians tearing down the fabric of the republic. Good Lord, what could you expect? The first chancellor of the Republic, Friedrich Ebert, had been a saddle maker.

The postwar years were both bleak and turbulent. The

political spectrum arced from extreme right to extreme left. Oratory took on a life of its own until the words destroyed the spirit of compromise so necessary in a parliamentary system, particularly one that included such widely, often wildly, divergent parties. The cost of the war and of the peace resulted in heavy tax burdens, which were frequently ruinous to members of the lower middle class. Theirs was a double loss, social and financial. To be pulled down to the level of laborers was an emotional trauma, often multiplied when unrestrained Inflation wiped out middle class savings. Opportunities to regain lost status were minimal, since high unemployment left so many willing hands and minds in angry idleness. Many of the small farmers, particularly those who had eked out a marginal existence, were unable to meet their mortgage payments. For many the ever-present fear of foreclosure became a reality. The newly dispossessed joined the ranks of the unemployed at the very time that even skilled workers were on the dole. No wonder the Wilhelmine days of fond recollections seemed like paradise lost to some, while others dreamed of the great new order promised by radical politicians.

Winzig survived the 1920s without the calamity of starvation. The new mayor replacing the ill-fated Krause was Walter Aust, a well-qualified and popular choice. Before coming to Winzig, he had been a secretary in the justice department, and his scholarly, soft-spoken demeanor offended no one. His mildly liberal views made him welcome among the farmers, merchants, and the few professionals. Despite the hard times, he was able to effect some improvements. He updated the Lustwald facilities, saw to the paving of major roads, and extended electric lighting.[1] In 1928, after ten years of austerity, the economic malaise appeared to be lifting, and finally it was reasonable to hope that the worst was over. And then the depression swept across the land. Unemployment figures soared, even in agricultural regions like Winzig. Field hands, apprentices, and clerks were dismissed as businesses shrank or went under. Das Weisse Ross, a tavern on Wohlauer Vorstadt, was converted into an unemployment office. The queue of the *Staemplers* (the unemployed, who were required to have a stamp entered into their dole book every week) grew longer and their mood more frustrated. Of course, the government was blamed, and this latest crisis fueled the political unrest that four years later enabled the Nazis to rise to power.

Winzig's political life was traditionally dominated by the rightist/conservative umbrella organization known as the Stahlhelm. As one might presume from the name, the "Steel Helmets," veterans of World War I, played a major role in this nationwide association. Its founder, Franz Seldte, stated the aim of his organization bluntly enough when he called for the mobilization of the spirit of the front-soldiers against the swinish Revolution. The swinish Revolution to which he referred was the overthrow of the monarchy and birth of the republic. The Stahlhelmers were avowed enemies of the communists as well as of the democratic parties. Their paramilitary trappings were as widely appealing (2 million members in 1920) as were promises to restore the old order.[2] A much smaller number of Winzigers supported the opposing alliance of prodemocratic parties, the Reichsbanner Schwarz-Rot-Gold. This coalition of democratic and socialist sympathizers was, however, never in a position of strength in rural Silesia.[3] The Reichsbanner could appeal neither to tradition nor sentimentality, vital ingredients of the allure of the right. There was no Communist party organization in Winzig.

The opening years of the 1930s witnessed the death of the Weimar Republic. A succession of socialist governments failed to alleviate the distress of the German people. Chancellor Heinrich Bruening, head of the Catholic Center party, tried in 1930 to restore some measure of economic stability but was unable to obtain a working majority in the Reichstag. He then hoped to avoid a complete paralysis of the state by requesting the application of the famous, or infamous, Article 48 of the Weimar Constitution. This provision permitted the suspension of parliamentary government in the case of a national emergency. The signature of the president was required to legitimatize such a moratorium on representative authority. The revered old soldier, President von Hindenburg, refused to sign and withstood Bruening's pressure. Bruening, valiantly but vainly, tried to steer the doomed republic through the tangle of acrimonious opposition from the right and the left. His policies earned for him the epithet of *Hunger Kanzler* as unemployment compensation ran out for millions of workers.

Hitler was so encouraged by his 1930 success in the Reichstag election, a gain of 6 million votes, that he decided to challenge von Hindenburg in the presidential campaign of 1932. Under the Weimar Constitution the president was given considerable power: his term in office lasted seven years; he could conduct foreign policy, command the armed forces, dissolve the legislature, the Reichstag, and call for new elections. No wonder Hitler used every means at his disposal to unseat the old marshal, while the supporters of von Hindenburg fought with equal determination to prevent a Nazi victory.

The political contortions of that contest validate the adage concerning strange bedfellows sleeping together. The Nazis joined with their most despised opponents, the Communists, to destroy *das System*. Both parties, of course, expected to feed on the carcass of the fallen republic. Von Hindenburg, whose very name symbolized the old guard, found himself the hope of the supporters of democratic government. Hindenburg was eighty-four years old in 1932. A father figure to many Germans, respected hero of the successful Russian campaign of the First World War, he was an ardent nationalist and monarchist whose heart belonged to Wilhelm. At best he was a conservative, at worst a reactionary, but by no stretch of the political imagination could he be labeled a liberal. There might be some justification to challenge his inclusion in the Prussian Junker class, but certainly he was a friend of that landowning military clique.

How remarkable indeed to find this Protestant monarchist seeking and receiving the support of the Catholic Center party, of the labor unions, of various democratic organizations, and even of the socialists. He, who had always viewed the Weimar Constitution with a great deal of skepticism, found himself its champion. Von Hindenburg regarded the possibility of Hitler in the presidential chair with such distaste that he willingly accepted help from any quarter. He was a soldier and his country needed him; he would not shrink from his duty. Hitler, on the other hand, had courted and won endorsement with an equally implausible alignment. An Austrian Catholic, a man totally lacking any qualifications for public service, uneducated, untrained, with an unpredictable personality, without a decent family background, and surrounded by questionable characters, he nevertheless obtained support from barons of industry and from segments of the military and the aristocracy. His greatest numerical strength came from the lower classes, but much of the money required for political campaigning came from wealthy Germans. Odd, but these rich and powerful members of the industrial and military aristocracy supported the Nazi party, although they would have been reluctant to invite Hitler into their drawing rooms. Hatred for the constitutional government drew them to the Austrian corporal, and in their vanity these barons from the Ruhr and the officer corps were convinced that Hitler could be manipulated by their superior power, will, and intelligence.

The political muddle of 1932 was further tangled by the action of the Stahlhelm organization. Marshal von Hindenburg was the honorary commander of this nationalist-rightist-conservative conglomerate, yet the Steel Helmets refused to endorse their own chief. They could not stomach the company he was keeping and ran their own candidate, Theodor Duesterberg, their second in command.[4] Thus, traditional differences between conservative, center, and liberal politics were blurred and the German voter was perplexed and repelled.

Analyses of the election results indicate that voters in the eastern areas of Germany, those nearest the Polish Corridor, found Hitler's fervent nationalism particularly appealing. The *Diktat* of Versailles was so unpopular that many conservatives were willing to ignore the unwanted components of Nazi ideology and vote for the man who promised to restore German pride. Other parties addressed themselves to the revision of the Treaty, but they could not produce a Hitler.

Generally, small-town politics had involved local issues. Interest in national elections waxed for a few weeks during the campaigns and waned as soon as the results were announced. In the two years between 1932 and 1934, however, the voters were given no respite. Five elections, uninterrupted rhetoric, attack and counterattack pitched the nation into a state of political fever. The utilization of the radio added a new dimension to oratory, and the Nazis were quick to see its possibilities. The impassioned appeals of Hitler and Goebbels echoed not only in homes and workplaces but also in public squares from loudspeakers. In many cities and towns the battle for voters crossed the line from angry words to physical combat. The use of weapons became less restrained as Reichsbanner members and Stahlhelmers and Communists clashed in the streets. The Nazi Brownshirts were delighted to enter the fray and prove their courage by breaking heads and bloodying noses. The nation seethed in a state of agitation that boiled over into political warfare all too often, all too quickly. The police seemed incapable of keeping peace, and the voters yearned for law and order. Even Winzig was not immune to the national aberration. The men who had the price of a beer disputed political issues at the saloons, and those with nothing but time to spend clashed with each other on street corners.

During the winter of 1932 the steps leading to the Steinhardt house were bloodied one night, the result of a political knifing. More often than not, fists and sticks underlined the points of the disputes. How was one to vote? Few Winzigers were National Socialists (Nazis); even fewer were socialists and democrats. Supporters of these political parties had no problem choosing their candidates. Most of the men (women rarely voiced political opinions before the Nazis came to power) held views that combined a strong sense of nationalism with an equally deep conservatism. The quandary of Hugo Kliem was typical. In the past his monarchist spirit had been at peace with von Hindenburg, but that was not possible in 1932, when the marshal courted the abhorrent labor unions, the socialists and the democrats. Cast your ballot for the Stahlhelm candidate, Duesterberg? Kliem was essentially in accord with his objectives, but the man had no chance to win the election and it was pointless to waste one's vote. The Communist candidate Thaelmann, was, of course, never a consideration. What about this Hitler then? He sounded like a man who would get things done, the sort of man the country needed. But he was an upstart, untried, unproved, and his anti-Semitic rhetoric was repugnant. Obviously, this Hitler did not know Jews as Kliem did, or perhaps the Jew baiting was merely a stratagem to appeal to the ignorant rabble. Night after night Hugo appeared at the home of his good friends, the Steinhardts, and pounded their kitchen table in frustration.

The results of the March elections are well known: von Hindenburg polled 49.6 percent and Hitler 30.1 percent. A month later, in the required runoff election, the voters gave von Hindenburg the necessary majority, 53 percent, while Hitler improved his total to 36.8 percent.[5] Winzig's statistics are not available. During the first week of the Soviet invasion the city hall was burned to the ground and Winzig's records went up in flames. But the loss of the archives matters little. Such documents could not give an accurate picture of the political convictions of the German people, neither on the national nor on the local level. The polling places were swarming with uniformed Nazis, members of the Sturmabteilung, the SA, who intimidated the voters with threats, fists, and clubs. The brown-shirted toughs stood by the ballot boxes, and when a voter refused to cast his ballot for Hitler he was beaten. Those standing in line, waiting to vote, knew what awaited them.

The Nazis were not yet in complete control of the election, but in many places a vote for von Hindenburg took moral and physical courage. Hitler's defeat in 1932 deserves to be considered the last victory of decency in the Reich before the era of darkness descended on the nation.

An incident in the hamlet of Pantken, some two miles from Winzig, illustrated the poisoned atmosphere of the early 1930s. After the election, Pantken's leading Nazi proudly announced that the entire village had voted for Hitler's NSDAP. But the farmer Theodor Nitschke knew better-he had voted for von Hindenburg. He told one and all that the election had been a swindle. In the evening, at the beer hall, he expressed his contempt in picturesque Silesian dialect, identifying Adolf's boys as *Schweinehunde* and dung cattle. He did not reach his home that night. He was arrested on Pantken's single street, and for three weeks no one knew what had happened to him. Suddenly he returned, a sullen, silent man who kept his own counsel and trusted no one.

The macabre death ritual of the Republic was not yet over. In May of 1933 the German people were asked once more to go to the polls, this time to elect a new Reichstag. Chancellor Bruening had resigned when von Hindenburg refused to sanction any further emergency decrees. Franz von Papen, the mediocre Talleyrand of Germany, whose politics were to the far right of center, created a new government. He was convinced that new parliamentary elections would give him the safe

majority he needed in order to enact legislation. The Nazis, he
thought, had passed their peak of popularity. Once more the
Brownshirts of the SA threatened voters, and it is impossible
to pass judgment on the validity of the results. The statistics,
however arrived at, gave the Nazis their greatest majority. No
other party could match their 230 seats in the Reichstag. Von
Papen's gamble had failed. Hitler was hopeful that his turn as
chancellor had come, that von Hindenburg would ask him to
form the next government. But the old president could not bear
the thought of dealing with Hitler. Von Papen used this
reprieve to offer Hitler a post in his government, but Hitler
refused. He would be chancellor or nothing! Then von Papen,
twisting and turning to retain some influence, persuaded the
marshal that the strength of the Nazis could be sapped if their
money supply dried up. He called on the men whose wealth
sustained the Nazi movement and achieved some success in
curtailing the flow of money from the giants of industry into
the Nazi coffers. Again he called for new Reichstag elections.
He hoped that a weakened Nazi party might induce Hitler to
participate in a von Papen government or, better yet, allow him
to govern without the Nazis.

When the results showed a loss of thirty-four seats for the
NSDAP, von Papen's shifty tactics seemed to be vindicated.
But then he overplayed his hand. He demanded changes in the
Reich's constitution that were unacceptable to the president.
Von Papen was replaced by Gen. Kurt von Schleicher who had
played a brief and despicable Machiavellian role in the making
and shaking of cabinets during the last two years of Hinden-
burg's presidency. His intrigues were to cost him his life in
Hitler's 1934 blood purge.

On January 28, 1933, after eight weeks in office, Schleicher
resigned. Von Papen, never far from the seat of power, agreed
to form a coalition government with the Nazis. Hitler became
chancellor, von Papen would be his vice chancellor. Von Papen
was neither the first nor the last man to delude himself that he,
a wealthy member of the aristocracy and an old hand in
politics, could manipulate Hitler. Von Hindenburg would have
to agree. The old man had to be convinced that there was no
other way out of the current dilemma but to ask Hitler to form
a government. The tactics employed by the pro-Nazi clique to

bring the feeble, probably somewhat senile, von Hindenburg
into agreement belong in the plot of a bad novel. Thus the die
was cast. On January 30, 1933, a jubilant Hitler achieved his
goal. Wrapped in the flag of the republic he despised, Hitler
became the legal chancellor of Germany.

The rapid Nazification of every stronghold of political,
economic, and cultural power was achieved without serious
challenge from the opposition parties. Forceful resistance could
have been expected from the revolutionary left. But the Nazis
removed the Communist threat in an action of unprecedented
political sleight of hand. There is little doubt that the Nazis
were responsible for setting the fire that destroyed the
Reichstag building. But immediately, before the ashes cooled,
the Communists were blamed. The government claimed that
the fire was an attempt to destroy the legitimate government of
Germany. Those who were guilty, the Communists, represented
a danger that could no longer be tolerated. Von Hindenburg
was pushed to invoke Article 48 of the Weimar Constitution.
Civil liberties were suspended, and a Communist witch-hunt
was orchestrated. Its party leaders were imprisoned or killed, its
presses smashed, its Reichstag members ousted. The Weimar
Republic had destroyed itself. The Social Democratic party
made a faint and belated attempt to stave off the republic's
death sentence. When Hitler demanded passage of the Enabling
Act, which gave him dictatorial power for four years, ninety-
four Social Democrats refused to endorse this final step toward
Fascism. But the law passed handily. Thus the claim by the
Nazis that their regime was legally constituted has a certain
merit. The adage that evil happens when good men do nothing
comes to mind.

How did the Nazis come to power in Winzig? Three
Winzigers, Lang, Schaube, and Juerke, emerged to become the
controlling trio during the next twelve years. They had joined
the NSDAP not during the party's early struggles, but when its
chances of success had increased between 1930 and 1933. Lang
had an unsavory past. Most recently he had risen from hawking
merchandise at the fair to earning his livelihood as a "nature
healer." He diagnosed illness by gazing into the eyes of the
poor and desperately ill and prescribed tonics and herbs. It was,
however, common knowledge that he derived his real income

from performing abortions. A typical scum that rose to the top, he had no legitimate business, no education, no profession, no respect from his peers. He found his identity and his place in society through membership in the Nazi party.

In August 1932, he founded the local party and became its leader (*Ortsgruppenleiter*). He could hardly claim to be an old fighter, as the early members of the NSDAP called themselves. Still, in Winzig he was a pioneer, willing to incur the aversion of the conservative community. Under the Fascist principle of leadership that linked political and administrative functions, he was appointed as Winzig's mayor by the Silesian district party leader (*Gauleiter*) in 1933.[6]

The number two man, Amtsgerichtsrat (magistrate) Schaube, came from a different world entirely. He was an educated man, a member of the professional class, a former judge of the local court. How did a man like that associate himself with the disreputable Lang? The simple characterization of opportunist does not fit him. Walter Wittmann, in his memoirs of Winzig, recalls that Schaube was the only idealist of the threesome, a man of deep religious faith, earnest, hardworking, and capable of total commitment to a cause. He was, perhaps, the sort of man who, had he lived in the Middle Ages, would have been a sorrowful yet efficient torturer for the Court of the Inquisition. In Winzig his role was less demanding. He became the town administrator and ran the day-to-day functions of government. He was also the legal counsel for the party and regarded as the actual power behind Lang's tainted throne.[7]

Juerke, the least important of the triumvirate, was nicknamed the Moor because of his swarthy complexion. His schooling had ended before he completed the elementary grades. He had made his living as a grave digger. In 1933 he became the town's vice mayor. Even with that impressive title he remained a nonentity, the butt of jokes and subject of raised eyebrows.[8]

The town council elections of 1933 provided interesting results. Of the fifteen members chosen, the NSDAP won three places. Winzig was still preserving its traditional conservatism. Although the Nazis made up only one-fifth of the council membership, they claimed the most important post of chairman for themselves. This was clearly a usurpation of power and, ominously and significantly, nothing was done to protest this action.

Neither Wittmann nor other Winzigers could explain why this unprecedented maneuver was not challenged. With the wisdom of hindsight, however, one can see the specter of brown-shirted toughs standing behind the Nazis on the council.[9]

Winzig's SA had begun humbly enough. Shortly after Lang established the local Nazi cell, a tailor named Cebulla put down his needle and picked up the shiny boots and Sam Browne belt. He was given official sanction to organize Winzig's Schutzabteilung. Most of his recruits were poor and unemployed. They risked nothing by joining. A uniform, even a partial one, offered status. The marching, the meetings, the shouting of slogans, the singing, and the occasional duties filled their time pleasantly enough. Payment for this political semimilitary army was irregular, but membership promised preferred status for employment. If the townspeople snickered, so be it. Soon enough their growing ranks would instill fear instead of sneers. Indeed, when the Nazis rose to national power in 1933 and when Goering ousted the elected socialist government of Prussia shortly thereafter, the tailor's troops were no longer a source of amusement to the people of Winzig. Their imitation of military discipline was offensive to the "real" soldiers of Germany. At first they seemed innocuous enough, crude boys posing as men, parading around town and singing a disgraceful new anthem. Something needed to be done to expose this masquerade. Surely the Stahlhelm leadership would order a showdown with these brown-shirted hooligans who would be taught an unforgettable lesson. The myth of the fighting ability of the Stahlhelm had inadvertently been fostered by the Nazi party leadership. The SA had instructions to avoid confrontations with the Steel Helmets, whose membership was greater and whose organization was believed to be superior. Also, the link between the Stahlhelm and the regular army was well known. Hitler had no wish to antagonize the army; his position was not yet sufficiently secure to take on such a risk.

Winzig's proximity to the Polish border gave the Stahlhelm additional importance. A special unit called the Grenzschutz, or Border Guard, had been established to provide protection against a possible Polish attack. These units were composed of

World War I veterans and theoretically had no political affiliation. In reality, they were indistinguishable from the Stahlhelm. The people of Winzig, like millions of conservatives throughout Germany, were waiting for the order from the Stahlhelm central office to face the SA. They expected, hoped for, an open battle to demonstrate their superiority once and for all. Obviously, the veterans of the First World War would put the SA to ignoble flight and then the Nazi rabble would learn the meaning of humility. But discipline required that the command be issued by the proper authority. An army, even such a semipolitical, semimilitary one, does not take matters into its own hands. Meanwhile, one must wait and not lose faith or courage.

As late as 1935, Winzig was buzzing with the telling and retelling of the incidents involving encounters between the two groups. For example, during the summer of 1934 the Stahlhelm and the Grenzschutz had assembled at the beer garden in the forest. A Major Neumann was in charge. He was making an appeal for the recruitment of new members when Lang and Schaube, both in brown uniforms, broke in on the meeting. They began to heckle the speaker, who, when he could no longer ignore the disruption, faced them and without a word pointed to the army insignia on his chest. After a long silence, Schaube read the warning implied in the gesture. He began to stammer and grew more confused, and both he and Lang turned and quickly left.[10]

A more serious clash took place in the following year. Walter Wittmann, a participant in the events, gave the following account: The city of Glogau was the host to the regional leaders of the Stahlhelm. From our area the grocer Puschmann, the innkeeper Kiesewetter, the master builder Schlichting, and I attended. On the way home we stopped in Steinau, where we went to a restaurant on Broad Street. Sitting there were a few half-drunk fellows who turned out to be "old fighters" of the SA. They insulted us and we threw them out. After the most obnoxious of the rowdies was flung into the street, Kiesewetter and I followed him and gave him a special beating. On the following day, it was claimed that he lay in the hospital with a concussion of the brain. But he recovered remarkably fast, in just a few days.

This incident resulted in a legal proceeding of the SA's Standart 51, Steinau, versus Puschmann et. al. We asked Dr. Joppich to defend us. Through a cousin of Schlichting's, a justice on a high court, we learned that our case looked bad. It was likely that the SA was planning to exploit this affair. That meant that we had to settle things according to our own ideas. We went to see the "old fighter" of the SA and, using our most persuasive cunning, we bribed him. We even wrote a receipt for the bribe on the back of a beer glass coaster. That piece of evidence we stuck under Schaube's nose and he did not like it in the least. At any rate, the court hearing was canceled. The Steinau SA commander, who used to be a gardener's helper, had to pull in his horns.[11]

That was in 1935. The date of this episode is interesting in view of the widely held impression that from the moment of Hitler's ascent to power Germany became an impregnable police state. In fact, between 1932 and 1934 Winzig took on the look of a comic opera set. The uniform craze was in full swing. There were the Nazis in brown, the Stahlhelm in gray, and the Reichsbanner folk in bits and pieces of World War I vintage. Some Winzigers wore their firemen's parade uniforms. The town council caught the fever and strutted about in ceremonial gold braid.[12] If the atmosphere had not been so full of tension, the scene would have been a farce. The long expected showdown between the Nazis and Stahlhelm never materialized. The question of this failure to act when the totalitarian designs of the new regime were abundantly clear deserves a closer examination.

The Stahlhelm had been founded as a fraternal, non-political organization of war veterans. The original intent was soon abandoned to counter the threat from the left, the "Red Danger" of Bolshevism and communism. The organization's popularity and power were based on several elements. Its right-wing politics suited the conservatives, and its link with the regular army conferred exalted status to its ranks. Its anti-Weimar stance appealed to the discontented, and its monarchist leaning fed the yearning for the life that was forever lost. The mantle of patriotism was of special importance in Silesia, where fear of an "imminent attack" by Poland circulated frequently and the Stahlhelm and Grenzschutz were seen as the first line of defense.[13] The leaders of the Stahlhelm realized that on several important points their policies coincided with those of the Nazis. Both wanted to renounce the Treaty of Versailles. Both held the republic in disdain. Both wanted to remilitarize the nation. Both hated communism with competing passion. Both organizations idolized and idealized the German past. Beginning in 1934, the Stahlhelm permitted nonveterans to join, but this innovation did not alter "the emphasis on the so-called soldierly virtues of discipline, heroism, manliness, etc."[14] Even their table of organization paralleled that of the NSDAP. Young members were inducted into the Scharnhorst troops. Their training, with an emphasis on discipline, continued until the young men achieved full membership. It is clear that the Stahlhelm leadership found it difficult to disavow the Nazis absolutely.

The political ambiguity in facing the Nazis was not the only weakness of the Stahlhelmers. Their commander, Duesterberg, was dropped because he had a Jewish ancestor. It was necessary to explain the resignation of their leader to the membership, and a Freiherr Grote undertook that task. Perhaps with tongue in cheek, he declared that said Jewish ancestor had won the Iron Cross during the War of Liberation in 1813, when he served as an eighteen-year-old volunteer, and "in those days Iron Crosses were harder to come by than in more recent times." The article concluded with a plea to Hitler to clarify once and for all the status of the Stahlhelm as separate but equal with the SA.[15] Instead of clarification, the Stahlhelm was consigned to absorption. The process began when Franz Seldte, the new commander, entered Hitler's first cabinet, claiming that he found himself at one with Hitler.[16] A decree, issued shortly thereafter, automatically enrolled the members of the Stahlhelm in the Nazi party.[17] If that order raised objections, they were inaudible. And action does not arise when curses are whispered to the walls.

Winzig surrendered to the Nazis the way all of Germany stumbled into the abyss; without a struggle. The rationale for such servility differed from group to group. The class-conscious bourgeoisie refused to believe that their inferiors could pose a threat to the established order. Civil servants, trained to obey rather than act independently, would not oppose instructions as long as the papers displayed the proper seals and signatures. The political opposition parties, ranging from socialists to democrats, failed to provide a leader who was both charismatic and courageous. Men of power and influence were certain Hitler could be taught to do their bidding. Consequently, the anti-Nazi masses remained voiceless and shapeless.

The German experiment with democratic republicanism died with merely a sigh. In Winzig the town council permitted a Nazi to sit at the head of the table although only some 20 percent of the people supported Hitler. Of course, small, insignificant communities had no chance at all to assert their political preference in the face of general acquiescence. That, indeed, is true. One supposes that the remembrance of that impotency, ("what could we have done?") consoled the council members and their equivalents all over Germany in the tragic years to come. Much consolation would be needed, not only by Germans, but people all over the world.

3

Something Ventured,
Nothing Gained

While the big shots have time and money to spare
Our troubles grow greater and harder to bear.
The drones sit snugly in city hall,
Who knows how we shall pay for it all?
Morals and decency have flown from sight
While plain folk toil from morn to night.
Expecting maiden, you want to be slim?
For just three marks, brother Lang makes you trim.
Vice and evil go without correction
Because the Nazi party gives its protection.
Our streets are renamed for celebrities new
Who dishonor our heroes old and true.
Please, let Winzig's big shots, Adolf great,
Share in Roehm's and Heines' fate.[1]
Without malice or rancor, we implore,
Deliver us to Reich Number Four.
Then on top of Branden Hill we will light
A bonfire of thanks and delight.[2]

These verses had been hand printed on a large piece of
cardboard suspended from the top of the pump that stood
between the Kliem and Steinhardt houses on the Vorstadt.
News of the poem spread quickly. An excited little group
gathered, and quickly the words were copied by several
onlookers. There were smiles and laughter and compliments for

the unknown author.

Within the hour the trio at city hall got wind of the "outrage" and the offending verses were taken to the mayor's office. Lang and Schaube were furious and determined to find the culprit.

That year, 1934, had been critical for Hitler; it was the year of the blood purge, "the night of the Long Knives". Hitler personally had ordered and participated in the murders of a number of his long standing comrades in the Nazi movement. Leaders of the SA were targeted specifically. The assassinations were carried out by the smaller elitist Blackshirts, the Schutzstaffel. The SS had originated as Hitler's personal bodyguard but was eager to expand its activities. Cutting down the competition gave them access to power, power that within a few years would exceed that of any other organization. Estimates of the number of murders committed that night range from 73 to 1,000. The action had no legal basis. There were no accusations, no trials, and no verdicts. Doors were burst open in the middle of the night, guns or knives drawn and men died. The explanation offered by the government, that the victims were homosexual and/or were engaged in a plot to overthrow Hitler, rang hollow. But there was no outcry for justice. The rule of law was already extinguished. The events of June 30 caused glee among the anti-Nazis and a moment of nervousness among the Nazis. Silesia was particularly vulnerable to criticism. Everywhere in Germany the SS had carried out the executions within the parameters of its orders, but in Silesia the troops had engaged in a private rampage of killing. In light of these circumstances, it is likely that Lang and Schaube felt compelled to flex their official muscle.

Both men were sensitive to their poor standing in the community. Exposure and punishment of the author of the "poem on the pump" might enhance their prestige. So the reluctant officer Urban was sent to fetch the town's best known anti-Nazis and bring them to city hall. There the suspects were given paper and pencil and told to block print one of the words appearing in the verse. Walter Wittmann was among those under suspicion. Usually unflappable, he was unnerved by the encounter at city hall. Schaube shook with rage as he shouted threats and accused Wittmann of high treason against the fatherland. But neither Wittmann nor anyone else knew the identity of the author. It was not until 1967 that Father Willinek, the Catholic priest, learned that the verses had been composed by his brother, Ernst.

A picture of life in Winzig between 1933 and 1940 should be painted in muted colors, neither in violent reds nor dull grays. Excluding the experiences of the Jewish families, there was a good deal of discontent but no actual suffering. When it became clear that the government's totalitarian tentacles were reaching into every home and workplace, the voices of open criticism were silenced. But the widely held impression that Germany, almost overnight, became a vast concentration camp is false. Equally erroneous is the opposite assessment which views the German people as hypnotized, shouting "Heil Hitler!" while goose-stepping in perfect unison.

Membership in the Nazi party and its satellite organizations increased in the next decade. The reasons for this expansion are as varied as the character of the individuals. Surely some Germans were deeply committed to the Nazi doctrines. They actually believed the theories and justified the activities of the regime. Others joined out of fear. Membership in the party granted protection from political and social harassment. But the desire for economic security was probably the most powerful driving force. The entire gamut, from real need to real greed, motivated hundreds of thousands to wear the swastika on their lapels. Advancement in the workplace, better housing, educational opportunities for the children, all were tied to Nazi party membership. Furthermore, since the party and the government were inseparable, existing associations were simply incorporated into the Nazi ranks. Professional, labor, and youth organizations found that, without consultation of the membership, they were incorporated into a Nazi affiliate.

The early years of Hitler brought some visible improvement to the nation. Most obvious was the reduction of unemployment and the disappearance of lawlessness from the streets. The fact that the government itself had become lawless was not nearly as perceptible. Beginning in 1933 legislation was enacted that provided jobs in the construction industry and extensive road building. During Hitler's first summer approximately 210,000 men went back on the payroll. By 1936 the number of unemployed, 7 million at its height, had been reduced to 1,500,000. The abolition of all labor unions was accomplished without serious protest in the face of this general economic recovery. The rise of hopes as well as income was discernable in every town and village.[3] Work on the Autobahn freeways and on secret defense installations along the Polish frontier shortened the line of jobless *Staemplers* in Winzig and by the late 1930s the unemployment office closed down.

The promise to rebuild the nation's agrarian base was partially fulfilled through a series of laws. In September 1934 primogeniture was recalled from the Middle Ages. Farms, to remain intact, were to be inherited by the oldest son. Younger sons and girls had to be content with whatever financial aid the parent chose to grant. Special courts were established to give relief to farmers in danger of foreclosure. These courts, in actuality, usually wiped out existing obligations.[4] Because many of Winzig's debt-ridden farmers felt more secure on their land, they moderated their anti-Nazi conservatism. The law also forbade landownership by Jews. Winzig's only Jewish farmer, Heymann Steinhardt, solved this dilemma by "selling" his acreage to his close friend Hugo Kliem and then leasing it back from him. In 1934 the Steinhardts still believed that they could outlast Hitler.

The educational system had been targeted as a priority for immediate change. The promised thousand-year Reich required intensive indoctrination of the children. Schools were the obvious medium to create the future race of super Germans. There was nothing subtle about the new direction for instruction. During the summer of 1933, "Heil Hitler!" was proclaimed the opening greeting for the school day.[5] Later that year, the usual morning prayer was discarded. Instead the students were instructed to recite a benediction of thanks to the fuehrer for saving the nation. A lesson was devoted to the proper method of giving the Nazi salutation: shoulders straight, feet together, right arm lifted straight out at a forty-five degree angle, then shout "Heil Hitler!" in perfect unison.

Georg Mai, an ardent Nazi, was the teacher in charge of Winzig's nine- to ten-year-old students. The class included two Jewish girls, the cousins Margot Moses and Rita Steinhardt. Dutifully they had followed his instructions when Mai became aware of their participation. He pointed his finger and said, "You two, remain seated and never say these words again!" He seemed to be very angry.

The girls were puzzled, and Margot asked, "Did we do anything wrong?"

Mai directed his answer to the class without a glance at the girls, "They are Jews. Not true Germans. An inferior race. We will learn more about this soon enough."

Margot and Rita exchanged wide-eyed looks of incomprehension.

Strict discipline had been the scaffolding of the Prussian educational structure, but the innovations now put into place went beyond the idealization of obedience. The recess period, previously an hour of individual play, was transformed into an exercise period, mainly marching and running. After 1935, the students used broomsticks to simulate guns as they circled the school yard again and again. Athletic excellence was valued over intellectual ability as the ideals of the *Official Handbook for Schooling the Hitler Youth* advanced into the classroom:

It is evident . . . that more attention be given to character training, of the will, to physical development, possibly less to objective training of the mind . . . thus the ideal of the young man is the good soldier. That of the young woman is the good mother.[6]

The National Education Ministry under the leadership of Dr. Bernard Rust, a former elementary school teacher, issued a flood of directives aimed at pounding German youth into the Nazi image.

In Hitler's own words, "the new generation must be slimmer and faster, swift as a greyhound and hard as Krupp steel."[7] With considerable imagination and total disregard for truth, every class lesson was pressed into the service of promoting Nazi ideology. *Rassenkunde*, the study of races, was the most blatant of the distortions.

The superiority of the so-called Aryans, the Germans in particular, was presented with a barrage of seemingly scientific data that the ordinary student had no reason to question. In Winzig, Miss Petzold, a bitter maiden lady who blossomed remarkably when she joined the ranks of the fanatical Nazis, told Rita Steinhardt (her hair was black, Margot Moses' merely brown) to come up to the front of the room. A blond, blue-eyed girl was then asked to come forward. With measuring tape in hand, the teacher compared the facial features of the two girls: nose, space between the eyes, ears, and so forth. She then posted the results on the blackboard. The differences between the Aryan and the Jew were, of course, quite remarkable and exactly as the textbook described. So there it was! The proven superiority of the Nordic type. Miss Petzold was rather delighted to carry out the mandate of the German History Education Department, which stated: "Make your point. Whether or not it is historically correct is not important."[8]

Geography included a 1936 atlas that showed "how crowded the German people live." Poland was depicted as a nation with equal numbers of Jews and Poles. A special illustration dealt with the German/Jewish question. A chart indicated that the previously accepted figure of 0.08 percent of Germany's population being Jews was wrong. The actual number was much greater, because Jews comprised a race, not a religion. According to the new calculations, over 1,500,000, that is, about 2 1/2 percent of the nation, was of the "Jewish race." The danger of such non-Aryan contamination was, of course, a constant theme in and out of German schoolrooms.[9]

The *Familienbuch* was an assignment required of all students. Boys and girls were directed to research their individual ancestry in order to establish their Aryan background. Family trees sprang up like mushrooms after the rain. Information concerning physical features, religious affiliation, occupation, service to the fatherland, and more had to be gathered from official records. Glory to him who found a fallen soldier in his past, but woe to the one who discovered a Jewish forebear. Proof of Aryan descent back to the year 1800 was a requirement for membership in the Nazi party.[10]

Highest honors were no longer awarded for academic achievement but were conferred for physical ability. The best athletes became the models of excellence. Acclaimed by the entire school, they were soon to be induced-or, more appropriately, seduced-into joining the Hitler Youth Movement. The number of uniformed boys and girls in the classrooms increased as membership opened doors to easy advancement.

During the first year or two of the Third Reich, Winzig's Catholics shared with their fellow Christians the false hope that their religious schools and practices were immune from persecution. The illusion was based on the concordat concluded with the pope in September of 1933 whereby the German government agreed to keep Catholic worship and all its institutions inviolate.

Father Willinek was Winzig's priest and the principal of its Catholic school. He was well liked, a man accepted by, rather than integrated, into Winzig's Protestant life. An able representative of his parishioners, he was conciliatory but not humble, self-assured but not aggressive. His success was evident when, in 1934, a new Catholic school was ceremoniously opened as a result of a joint effort between the church and the town. The former contributed two-thirds and the latter the rest of the required funds.

Before the year ended, however, the hope of Winzig's Catholics that their status would be respected was in doubt. The incident was a petty one, but Father Willinek quite correctly saw it as a straw in the wind indicating future directions. The Saar Province had voted to rejoin the German nation after fifteen years of French domination. Children from the Saar were invited to spend their holidays with German families. The priest had extracted a promise from the mayor that Catholic children would be placed in Catholic homes. But when the youngsters arrived, Mayor Lang reneged, saying, "There are no Protestant or Catholic children! Only German children!"

Willinek's protests were met with a shrug of the shoulders and the matter was closed.

Step by step the provisions of the concordat were violated. Catholic youth groups were outlawed. The Catholic press was stilled and Catholic schools were closed.[11] By 1939 Father Willinek was teaching students in secret. Several times a week he was seen bicycling to the homes of various congregants, supposedly visiting the old and the sick. Whether Lang or Schaube knew that the priest used these occasions to give religious instruction to small groups of children is a matter of conjecture. It is a fact, however, that he was not hindered in the pursuit of his calling throughout the Nazi years.

The paganism that was extolled by some members of the Nazi hierarchy was an extremism that found little support throughout the nation. Certainly the older generation exhibited no appetite for a return of Valhalla. Outwardly Christianity continued to be practiced by most Germans, but it was a spiritless, subservient faith that had abandoned the teaching of Jesus. The rituals were left, but the words of the Prince of Peace were drowned out by the rattling of the weapons of war. The tiny candle of Protestant anti-Nazi opposition was easily blown out. Pastor Niemoeller and his Confessing Church tried to rally Germans to live their faith. But, at most, his group comprised 15 percent of the German Evangelical Church. When Niemoeller was arrested and sent to various concentration camps, his movement faltered.

The Lutheran ministers formed an association in an attempt to retain the independence of their pulpits. Rather than fight the association openly, the Nazis made it ineffectual. They appointed one of their own creatures as bishop of the synod. Although an anti-Christian bias was part of youth group orientation, it was the government's policy to avoid as much as possible direct confrontations with the Protestant Church.[12]

So a stillness descended on the houses of worship. The buildings remained, the people sang hymns on Sunday and the holy days, but it was best, certainly safer, not to delve too deeply into the true message of the Christian faith. The mainstream of ministers exhibited no courage. Winzig's Pastor Boerner was not of the heroic mold. He complied with the general directives of the party, kept clear of politically critical topics in his sermons, and tried to ignore the uniformed men in the back row. His congregation had shrunk, most noticeable was the absence of young people. What was in his heart we cannot know.

The *Kinderfest*, usually accompanied by happy excitement, became controversial in 1934. There were only two Jewish children left in the public school, Margot and Rita. What bad luck! Margot won most of the athletic contests. She was entitled to the vaunted crown of the queen of the *Kinderfest*. The judges were in a quandary, while the Nazi dignitaries were outraged. There could be no Jewish royalty. But the school principal, Rektor Spieler, insisted. The rules were clear and

Margot stood her ground. She refused to abdicate her royal right! The Rektor declared her the rightful queen. After some difficulty, she found three other girls, in addition to her cousin Rita, to act as her maids of honor. In the evening, when the children paraded back to Winzig from the Lustwald, Margot walked under the cornflower crown with an air of resolution. The Nazis fumed and promised that such an affront would never be repeated. They were right. On the morning of the *Kinderfest* the following year, no queen walked beneath the flowered hoop. Margot and Rita stood behind a curtained window of their house and watched in silence.

Winzig's political life had its moments of melodrama during the thirties. The political waters were not as quiet as the weekly paper so endlessly proclaimed. Not even in Winzig. Resistance to the Nazi power structure came from two widely divergent sources-a man and a woman with very little in common. Neither would have conceded that their struggle against Lang and Schaube were in any way comparable. They were never friends. In fact, they moved in very different social circles. Both, however, had made assumptions that right actions will bring right results. They were wrong, of course.

The lady was tall and blond. She wore her hair in a braid twisted around her head, and she carried her large frame with a straight back and a purposeful stride. Her name was Martha Hildebrandt, but she was always called Hulda, a name that suited her *Walkuerian* bearing. Her husband owned the Black Eagle Inn on the Ring. Hulda was the dominant member of the pair, both in business and in their private lives. It was Hulda who would star in the "Hildebrandt affair" while Herr Hildebrandt was cast in a supporting role.

Hulda was one of the few Winzigers who could call herself an"old fighter," since she had joined the NSDAP before 1930. The Black Eagle, quite naturally, became a favorite gathering place for the local Nazi clique, and Hitler's victories were celebrated with countless steins of brew. Hulda, outspoken and completely at ease among the men, was a respected member of the group. But not for long.

When power had been transferred from Winzig's conservative leadership to the Lang and Schaube duo, Hulda was disappointed. She should have been jubilant; instead she became critical and sharply faultfinding. She was an idealist, uncompromising in the expectation that the new Germany would be led by warriors, men whose idealism matched her own. Behind the bar at the inn she displayed a picture of Hitler, always adorned with fresh flowers. The fuehrer's eyes seemed to admonish her to set things right in Winzig. Lang in particular, Schaube and Juerke to a lesser extent, did not meet her standards of government in the new Reich.

She heard and saw much as she served the tankards of beer at the inn. The mayor and his cohorts were no better, in fact much worse, than the pettifoggers they had replaced. Where she expected to see supermen, she found only self-serving bunglers. Her indignation was fueled by rumors of mismanagement of funds, of the wrongful use of the official car, tales of stupidity and abuse of power. Hulda could not stand by while Winzigers sneered at the Nazi administration. This was an intolerable state of affairs that she must set right. So she became an informer. The county officials were kept abreast of every infraction she could charge against Winzig's administrators. Her accusations grew into a bombardment of letters and phone calls. She traveled to the county seat in Wohlau to file her complaints in person. But she was ignored, and no action was taken.[13] In the world of reality, Nazi officials were not eager to make enemies of comrades based on the carping of an overzealous woman. Since Hulda made no secret of her intention to cleanse Winzig of its nest of drones, a small group of like-minded neighbors gathered about her. She was no longer a lone woman who "ought to stop meddling in men's affairs and get back into the kitchen." Among her intimates were several prominent members of the party: Dr. Mueller, the physician, and also Dr. Giesel, the dentist. These men, and others, shared in the embarrassment that the town was run by a former nature healer and a grave digger. It was unseemly, un-German, and created disrespect for the regime. The mayor and his friends were furious with Hulda, but other than declaring the Black Eagle out-of-bounds for the party faithful, there was nothing they could do. They probably hoped that Frau Hildebrandt would realize that she was unable to force the authorities to investigate her complaints. But they misjudged Hulda. Her failures merely aroused her passion to create her world in Hitler's image. The county, the Silesian district authorities, and the Prussian state bureau in charge of official misconduct continued to receive salvos of her angry protests. The townspeople, for the most part, watched with gleeful curiosity. One morning Hulda received a token of encouragement. One of the street signs had been painted over during the night to read "Huldaplatz."[14]

How many times did Hulda sigh, "If only the fuehrer knew . . ."

Clearly a new approach was needed. If the lower echelons of the party ignored her, well, there was only one thing left to do. She must tell the fuehrer. She must go to Berlin and place her grievance before the all-highest himself. In 1934 personal audiences were still granted by Hitler. Hulda went to work and set into motion the complicated machinery that made this possible. She persevered through the lengthy and trying screening process, and her persistence paid off — she was granted an audience.

With head and hopes held high, Hulda boarded the train to Berlin. Rektor Spieler, although not a party member, was privy to the events and recalled Frau Hildebrandt's account of this extraordinary day in her life:

> After several hours of waiting, one of Hitler's aides informed me that I would be permitted three or four minutes of the fuehrer's time. This was not enough for a presentation of my prepared indictment, but I was determined to do my utmost to set matters right in Winzig. I was ushered into Hitler's presence and his first question was unexpected:
>
> "Who paid for your trip to Berlin?"
>
> I answered that I had paid out of my own funds. Hitler seemed pleased and he then inquired into the purpose of my trip. As rapidly as I could, I described the situation in Winzig. Before I had finished, Hitler interrupted me with the comment that he did not have such local leaders in the Reich. He then extended his hand with the assurance that matters would be put in order. I handed him a written statement I had brought and said, "I guess this will end up in the wastebasket

with all the others."

Hitler reacted to this criticism with a sign of real interest. He rang for an aide, a certain von Blankenburg, and instructed him to give special attention to my problems and thanked me for coming. Already dismissed, I nonetheless fired one more shot on behalf of Winzig, "Why have we failed to receive an army garrison as did the neighboring towns?" Hitler replied that this was a subject I ought to discuss with the army ministry. And with that the audience was over.[15]

Hulda returned on a cloud of optimism. Redress was surely close at hand. Indeed, shortly after her trip, two gentlemen from Berlin arrived in town. They conducted interviews, took notes and left. Hulda and her friends congratulated one another, but their euphoria was short-lived. Days of waiting turned into weeks and then the weeks stretched into months. There simply was no further action.

The little group of dissidents was uncertain about continuing the struggle. Was it not time to get on with their lives? But Hulda would not hear of it; her determination had become an obsession. To their credit, her friends stood by her as she entered into the final phase of her battle to make Winzig representative of all she so naively assumed Nazi ideology had pledged.

After all the failures, the only remaining weapon against the scoundrels, the *Halunken*, was to bring them to court and charge them with abuse of office. Such a case would fall under the jurisdiction of the special courts of the NSDAP. The Nazis had established a separate administration of justice that dealt with party matters. Cases concerning such complaints as membership qualifications, party discipline, use of party funds, and so forth were tried here. The system consisted of a series of lower courts whose decisions could be appealed, if necessary, to a higher tribunal.[16] Hulda brought suit against Winzig's top three Nazi officials for behavior detrimental to the party and the fatherland. Her accusations were backed by a number of specific charges. She collected affidavits and depositions attesting to the malfeasance of the accused. The fact that she also had corroborating testimony from witnesses attested to her persuasive powers. A personal appearance in such a court was nerve-racking at best, dangerous at worst.

The court was convened in Wohlau. The county leader of the party, von Ridder, sat as judge. The issues of the case were represented and countered by the defendants over several sessions lasting twenty-three hours. Hulda presented a closely argued case against Lang, Schaube and Juerke. The trio used their position in their own, not the town's, best interest. The most startling appearance was that of the school principal, Rektor Spieler. Fortunately, the *Rektor* was a prudent man. Long ago he had established the habit of carefully recording events pertaining to his career. When, to his great surprise, he received a subpoena to appear, he made notes for use in his own testimony, and he also kept a record of the proceedings. His meticulousness permits the reconstruction of the trial which took place in 1935.

Spieler's appearance at the hearing chamber created quite a stir. Tall, thin, with iron gray hair and glasses, in his dark suit and white shirt, he was out of place among all the uniforms. He was the only person not dressed in party brown. The presiding official asked him if he was a member of the party. Spieler's "No" created more confusion. It was most unusual to have a nonmember appear at party court.

"Perhaps you prefer that I withdraw?" suggested the *Rektor*.

The court deliberated for a few moments and then requested that he stay. The charges were read: "Frau Hildebrandt, together with a number of respected party members, accuse these named officials of Winzig of misconduct, of lacking the higher principles of the NSDAP and of representing a danger to the Reich."[17] Spieler was asked to take the stand. Because he was well aware that his evidence might be altered to conform with the outcome of the trial, he had made some preparations. He now said: "I will speak only if certain of my conditions are met."

The court was aghast: "We are not accustomed to have witnesses dictate conditions to us!"

"But I am not a party member, therefore the usual rules do not apply to me," Spieler replied.

Again heads were bent in consultation. Then the judge inquired into the nature of Spieler's conditions.

"First, I will speak only if my words are taken down by the court typist and if I will receive a copy of my statement at the conclusion of my testimony. Second, I wish to know beforehand how much time has been allotted to me."

Another hurried conference resulted from the *Rektor's* insistence on knowing how much time the court planned to allow for his testimony. The court requested to hear the reason for this demand.

"Because I have prepared my statement according to the limitations you may set for me. If you give me ten minutes, then I will read the lines I have marked in blue, if I have twenty minutes, then the paragraphs in red. Should there be no restraints on time, then I will read my entire paper."[18]

This time the magistrate and his associates withdrew to another room. After some moments they returned and declared themselves willing to permit Spieler to speak as long as he wished.

Spieler was on the stand for an hour and a half. His testimony concerned his own struggle with Winzig's leading Nazis. He had been defamed by them, hounded and persecuted. By means of treachery and trickery the three accused men had deprived him of his position as *Rektor* of Winzig's school, and their chicanery had very nearly cost him his health.

Upon conclusion of his statement, Spieler submitted the corroborating affidavits. Inasmuch as no one had asked him to leave he was able to observe the testimony of the next witness, Dr. Mueller.

From the witness stand the doctor pointed his finger at Lang and shouted, "Here sits our town leader! I know him to be guilty of three cases of illegal abortion!"

"Such an accusation must be supported," the judge admonished the doctor.

Thereupon Dr. Mueller placed sworn affidavits that attested to the facts of the charge upon the table. Von Ridder now declared that this issue was a criminal matter, not under the jurisdiction of a party court. He added that he would submit pertinent documents to the district attorney for further action.[19]

The two most serious indictments against the trio concerned mismanagement of public funds and misuse of authority. One of the lesser charges brought against Schaube was not without its ironic note. Schaube was accused of insincerity in his hatred of the Jews. Had he not lived, for a time, in the house of the Jewess Schlesinger? Had he not been seen in said Jewess's store buying children's clothing? If the court had questioned the Jewish families in Winzig, they could have exonerated the maligned Schaube, testifying to the fact that he persecuted them with complete devotion.

The trial was over. What was the verdict? Hulda, her friends and the rest of Winzig waited and waited and waited. At long last, even the most sanguine of her circle had to face the truth. There would be no verdict! Unofficially and obliquely a decision was rendered when von Ridder was removed as county leader of the party and replaced by none other than Winzig's Schaube.[20]

Hulda paid dearly for her romantic illusion of a Germany created in the image of Goebbels's propaganda campaigns. Her party membership was revoked. Then the Hildebrandts lost the inn. Soon thereafter they moved away.

1954, not long before her death, she received a letter from her old enemy, Schaube. He was dying but could not face his maker without her forgiveness for the wrong he had done her. He was contrite and full of remorse. Hulda accepted his penitence. Perhaps this kindness eased the final days for both, victim and victor of justice in the style of the Third Reich.[2]

With Hulda's defeat and the capitulation of the Stahlhelm, all open opposition against the Nazis in Winzig was ended. On an individual basis, however, conservative and NSDAP personalities continued to clash. There was, for example, the matter of the *Schandsaeule*, a tree trunk placed on the west side of the Ring. Schaube was said to have originated the idea of shaming so-called enemies of the Reich by publicly exposing their misdeeds. Only one inscription was ever placed on this Nazi version of the pillory. It referred to the local Stahlhelm leader and read: *"Walter Kahl — Deutsch Fatal."* Just why Walter was fatal to Germany was not very clear, even to Winzigers. One night some of the townsmen expressed their disapproval of the Schandsaeule by dousing it with tar. There was a good deal of huffing and puffing to bring the suspected Stahlhelmers to trial for the destruction of public property. But the county organization of the party had heard quite enough on that subject and suggested that the contentious column simply disappear. And so it did, Cebulla and his SA carried it off after dark. The mayor placed this new crime upon the convenient heads of the Stahlhelm. Hulda, however, knew better. She told one and all to look for the cursed pillar in the basement of party member Otto Schumann's house.[22]

Whereas most Winzigers regarded this incident as yet another example of official absurdity, the ordeal faced by their *Rektor* was another matter entirely. For two years Rektor Spieler, the head of the public school, battled the party for his job, his reputation, and his future. The attempt to discredit and remove him from office emanated from three sources.

Locally, Mayor Lang was on the attack and, in fact, had initiated the proceedings. On the next level, von Ridder's party organization had joined the battle, and finally, the county Nazi Teachers' Association aligned itself against Spieler. The teachers group was headed by Superintendent of Schools (Schulrat) Tretz, whose name was spoken with reverence because his son was a member of Hitler's personal bodyguard.

The Rektor's prolonged struggle, which he called his "battle against slander for honor and right," was the result indirectly of his democratic political views. But the fire and smoke of the case were produced by one of Winzig's teachers, Georg Mai. Mai was a Nazi. He was ambitious. He had money problems and he wanted Spieler's job. The mayor was eager to Nazify the town completely, to make it a model of conformity with the ideals of the new regime. To achieve this goal, all non-party members had to be removed from positions of authority. Spieler was one of the most visible and most respected men in Winzig. His very presence was a thorn in Lang's brown-shirted side. The mayor's desire dovetailed neatly with those of Mai, who was in the perfect position to attack the Rektor. If necessary, Mai could swear that Spieler's leadership of the school was out of step with the Third Reich. The alliance of Lang and Mai was clearly a matter of mutual need and shared hypocrisy.

Spieler had given Winzig twenty-five years of service. He had come as a teacher and been promoted to principal. His family life was exemplary. He had a devoted wife and two handsome children. They had built one of the town's showcase homes across the street from the school-a neat white house with colorful shutters and flowers all around. Spieler was an active citizen and had been involved in the politics of Reichsbanner Schwarz-Rot-Gold. He had acted as a consultant for the juvenile court and was an officer in the pre-Nazi teacher's union. When Lang became mayor, Spieler was vicechairman of the school board. In that capacity he collided with Lang, whose position automatically entitled him to be the chairman of the school board. Thus the board meetings became the stage for their conflict.[23]

Lang officiated at the meetings. He ignored Spieler completely, even refusing to acknowledge his existence. Consequently the *Rektor's* judgments were effectively blocked. Next, Lang moved to undermine Spieler's position. He circulated lists of complaints to all associations in which the *Rektor* held a membership. The reaction was predictable. Within a few months Spieler was removed from all the honorary and paid appointments save that as head of the school. All offices he vacated were filled by Mai!

But the mayor did not have the power to remove Spieler from his post. Such action was under the jurisdiction of the *Schulrat*, the superintendent of schools. It was clear that Lang expected Spieler would resign rather than endure continued harassment. But Spieler was not a willing victim. For months Mai had leveled accusations against his principal to the regional administrator. The educational system was dominated by Nazis, and the *Rektor* was refused the opportunity to answer the charges. In order to force a confrontation that would permit the accused to face his accusers, Spieler requested a disciplinary hearing-against himself! But the petition was denied, with the excuse that "there is no case against you."

Nevertheless, a few weeks later the *Schulrat*, Herr Daunert, called at Spieler's office. He placed before the Rektor a long list of charges. All were filed by Mai.

DAUNERT: I want your immediate comment on each of these charges.
SPIELER: That is impossible. But I will agree to a face-to-face confrontation with my accuser. This should be done in the presence of the faculty and the superintendent.
DAUNERT: Your request is denied.[24]

Spieler was able to delay Daunert long enough to make some notes and comments concerning the indictment:

1. The *Rektor* had displayed an un-German sympathy toward the Jewish children in Winzig. For example, he had permitted the itinerant Jewish religion teacher the use of his office for instruction. He had permitted a Jewish girl to be crowned at the *Kinderfest.* He had punished an Aryan boy for beating up a Jewish child, Siegfried Steinhardt.
   (All of the above charges were basically true.)
2. The *Rektor* had refused to fly the swastika from the school's flagpole after the election of 1932.
   (True. The school did not yet possess a Nazi flag.)
3. The minutes taken by Spieler when he was secretary of the teachers' association revealed anti-Nazi commentaries.
   (True. These were quotations from topics under discussion at the meetings.)
4. Spieler was a longtime Socialist.
   (Untrue. He was a democrat.)
5. Spieler conducted a patriotic assembly in the rear school yard instead of beneath the swastika in front of the building.
   (True. There was not enough room in front.)
6. Spieler replaced signs reading "Shut the door" with signs requesting, "Please, close the door." This revealed an un-Aryan attitude. Children must be commanded, not asked to obey.
   (No comment.)
7. Spieler had failed to attend a meeting featuring an important Nazi speaker.
   (True. His wife had collapsed that day at her mother's funeral.)
8. Spieler no longer had the confidence of the student body.
   (A lie.)

The *Rektor's* frustration over his inability to defend himself against the allegations was wearing him down. He found it particularly difficult to face Mai day after day. Physically and emotionally drained, he applied for and was granted a month's leave of absence. The county physician was aware of the stress and consented to five more months of sick leave.

The temporary withdrawal of the *Rektor*, however, settled nothing. A visit from the district leader of the Nazi Teachers' Association failed to bring about a solution. Once more, Mai's complaints were discussed and Spieler's defense fell on deaf ears. The district leader declared that, in essence, Mai was acting in the best interest of the party. Yes, on several counts the young teacher had been excessive and would be reprimanded. But that was all. A renewed request for disciplinary action by Spieler against himself was again rejected. He was not to have the opportunity to appear in a public forum. Spieler became ill. The strain was becoming unbearable, and he soon suffered a nervous breakdown. Steadfast friends and students eased his isolation for brief moments. One day a group of students noticed the *Rektor* at his open window. They set up a chant: "one, three, five, nine, our *Rektor* is just fine, two, four, six, eight, ten, and we want him back again."[25]

There could no longer be any doubt that the county school officials were more concerned with pleasing the party than with the merits of the case. When Spieler was well enough, he appealed to the next level of authority, the Provincial School Council, which had the power to override county decisions. But in order to get a hearing in Breslau, the detestable county *Schulrat* had to endorse the request. Daunert refused to give his permission. The rope tying the *Rektor's* hands was beginning to tighten like a noose. But not quite yet. Spieler used Daunert's rebuff as a wedge to pry open a door of the Provincial Education Department. Would someone explain what his remaining options were? Surprisingly, he was granted an interview by the head of the Silesian School Administration, Dr. Ruchatz. It was an astonishing meeting. Ruchatz proved to be representative of the best in the tradition of the German civil service. He was not a member of the party and as late as 1939 had not been removed from his position. Ruchatz was not impressed by political connections. He judged people and events on their merit. That such a man had retained his professional post was a small miracle. Finally, after so many rejections, Spieler found an official who listened with sympathy and increasing indignation. Ruchatz assured the *Rektor* that he would lift his petition from the net of personal intrigue and place it before the highest authority: the national minister of education, Rust. The *Rektor* addressed a bitterly worded demand, not a plea, for justice to Minister Rust in support of this action.

Once more, it was a time for waiting. Several weeks after Spieler's visit to Breslau, the long awaited reply arrived. The family gathered around to hear the verdict. Spieler read it and joined his wife and children in a joyful hallelujah. Rust's investigation resulted in a complete exoneration. All charges were dismissed. The minister concluded that it was unlikely that Spieler could derive any satisfaction from further service in Winzig and asked if he would accept the position of principal in the city of Guhrau. Since Guhrau had twice the population of Winzig, this transfer was, in fact, a promotion.[26] His vindication restored the *Rektor* in mind and body. He went to Guhrau to make the obligatory call on the mayor, followed by the amenities of protocol with the school authorities. He found a house and returned to Winzig to prepare for his move. But his enemies were not yet defeated. The news of Spieler's victory reached the party, and once again unseen wheels were set into motion. In the midst of packing for his relocation to Guhrau, the *Rektor* received the devastating news that the offer had been withdrawn. It was a blow that left Spieler close to despair. Such a long struggle, so many defeats, and now, with victory apparently assured, again he faced professional and personal ruin. The world had become unrecognizable. Those sworn to uphold justice had become agents of injustice. Why continue the hopeless contest? The well-informed Daunert (no doubt, Mai had kept him abreast of all developments concerning the *Rektor*) now requested a meeting with Spieler.

The two men confronted each other in a restaurant. Daunert, eager to exploit the *Rektor's* frame of mind, alternately offered him a carrot and showed him the stick:

The party is instituting a suit against you. Your action
against members of the NSDAP can be interpreted as
treachery. Specifically we have lodged the charge of
"seditious agitation against a personage of the state."
You have used up all possible sick leave. If you do not
go back to work, you will be dismissed. Perhaps you
should forget about school administration and return to
teaching. There is just one alternative to save you, a
position of principal in the town of Maltsch. Take that
and stop fighting so many windmills.[27]

Spieler said little. In the end, he wearily pushed aside the
cups and saucers on the table and signed his acceptance of the
offer. Maltsch was not a bad place, not very different from
Winzig. The students gave Spieler a farewell dinner. Friends
called to wish him and his family Godspeed and expressed
regrets to see them go. But the Spielers derived little pleasure
from these visits. They were too tired and heartsick. Essentially,
they had fought alone.

Few Winzigers appreciated the broader implication of
Spieler's removal from a job well done. After all, everyone had
troubles of his own. Everyone was busy. Especially Georg Mai.
He moved into the *Rektor's* office and ordered that signs on
the doors throughout the school be changed to a single word:
"SHUT."

Heymann Steinhardt. His patriotism, like that of many German Jews, was despised by the Nazis.

Rita Steinhardt in her early teens.

Walter Steinhardt in 1937, the year he escaped to England.

Sigfried Steinhardt in 1938.

Steinhardt and Moses cousins at a birthday party in May 1935. From right to left: Walter Steinhardt, Josef Moses, Josef Steinhardt, and two younger cousins.

Rektor Spieler, principal of Winzig's public school, whose decency was not acceptable to Nazi concepts of education.

Rita Steinhardt and Margot Moses's class at the Winzig public school in 1935. Margot Moses is second from the left in the back row; Rita Steinhardt is the last girl on the left in the middle row.

The Steinhardt/Moses complex.

The Steinhardt/Moses bakery, which stood on the corner, at the righthand side of the house.

The Steinhardt/Moses mill and barns, which stood on the lefthand side of the house.

Two views of Winzig in the 1930s.

Father Joseph Willinek, a Catholic priest in Winzig until 1945 and a leader of the town's population in exile. He was a founder of *Heimatklaenge*.

Dr. Mueller's house. It was the only house that remained on the west side of the Ring after the fires that occurred during the Russian invasion in 1945.

4

Anti-Semitism:
Blight and Flight

Most Germans seemed satisfied with the direction of national politics between 1933 and 1939. There was peace and the welcome perception of prosperity around the corner. A general atmosphere of optimism persuaded parents that their children would experience fewer hardships than they had suffered. Hitler's policies, domestic and foreign, had resulted in a string of extraordinary successes. Germany's international importance was enhanced, and her internal problems were swept from sight. By measures fair and foul, the economy was revived and unemployment decreased drastically. Lawlessness and fear of anarchy no longer plagued the citizenry as troublemakers disappeared off the streets. Hard work and long hours for little pay were better than idleness and the dole. It was an exciting time to be alive. Almost daily some exhilarating event confirmed the vision of a renewed Germany. Such a generalization is, of course, subject to the pitfalls inherent to all such sweeping statements. There were always Germans who hated the regime. Those few who actually fought the Nazis and those whose past affiliations made them suspect generally paid with their liberty or their lives. It is pertinent to remember that the original concentration camps were constructed for the political enemies of the Third Reich. The names in the Gestapo files that were first designated NN (*Nacht und Nebel*, night and fog) were anti-Nazi Germans, destined to disappear without a trace.

But opposition to the regime was never widespread. The majority of Germans accepted Hitler. With or without enthusiasm, they consented to the new agenda. Why? That will always be the haunting question. Why were the German people willing to submit to a dictatorship that not only deprived them of political freedom, but invaded their personal lives to an unprecedented degree? This government nullified traditional concepts of inheritance, marriage, child rearing, and occupational choices. The party claimed the right to decide who was a friend and who was an enemy, how leisure time should be spent, what to read, and where to shop. Passively, almost indifferently, the German people allowed their liberties to be usurped.

Much has been written about the Germans' idealization of obedience. For centuries patriotism had been equated with military discipline. The soldier who died in battle was paid greater homage than the paradigm among the living. Parents judged their children on the basis of compliance and submission. The good child obeyed without question. But surely other societies held similar values yet did not relinquish all ethical and moral standards. The economic hardships endured by the German people during the thirties were, by no means, unique. Poverty and hunger were worldwide problems. Was the need for a securely structured existence so compelling that, as Erich Fromm suggested, the Germans actually sought escape from freedom? One can only theorize that a number of different threads intertwined to create the ropes that bound a nation so willingly, almost eagerly, to submit to years of degradation.

Did most ordinary citizens actually share Hitler's image of the future? Did they support some, or many, of his policies? Did they believe in their own racial superiority? Did the vision of a prostrate Europe at Germany's feet represent their national ambitions? Did they believe the propaganda that depicted the Jews as their most catastrophic misfortune? How many would have cheered the fuehrer without the motivation of a better job, a more secure future for their children, or a good pension? It is impossible to assess the number of Germans who accepted Nazi ideology as a matter of conviction rather then convenience. Obviously, after the defeat of 1945, admitted Nazis were a rare breed. Even members of the party and the bureaucracy would claim, and in some cases truthfully, that they hated everything the Nazis stood for. But what could they do? They had families to support, obligations to meet.

On a national scale it is impossible to uncover the secret thoughts of millions of people, but the microcosm of Winzig allows for some conjecture. In a small town where gossip is the favorite form of entertainment, political convictions are hard to conceal. How did some Winzigers regard their fellow townspeople? The answers are not a scientific sampling, but they represent some well-informed estimates.

Heymann Steinhardt, the Jewish farmer who owned a mill and bakery in the Vorstadt, believed that one-third of Winzigers supported most Nazi policies. Another third he considered to be realists who heiled Hitler without either shame or fervor because they hoped to protect their economic interests. The final third saluted the fuehrer through gritted teeth, usually silent in their opposition. His sister, Anna Moses, an especially keen judge of character, numbered the active Nazis to comprise about 20 percent. She divided the remaining 80 percent between the politically neutral and the covertly opposed. As Jews, Heymann and Anna not only observed changes among their neighbors, they also experienced them. Who continued to greet them and who looked away? Who visited during daylight and who came after dark? Who encouraged the abuse of the Jewish children and who tried to stop it? Who maintained a business relationship and who ended it? Who paid his debts and who refused?

Rektor Spieler, a Protestant and member of Winzig's professional class, saw a somewhat different picture. In his estimate only one in a hundred townspeople approved of Hitler completely. Of course, "approve completely," excluded the Nazis who supported some, though not all, of Hitler's policies. Only 5 percent of Winzigers joined the party of their own free will, but Spieler concluded that even among this small number, economic rather than political considerations predominated.

Father Willinek, the Catholic priest, had yet another point of view. The members of his congregation had witnessed the anti-Catholic bias of the Third Reich. In the father's judgment, not more than 5 percent of the townspeople were dedicated followers of the Nazi dogma. Despite considerable pressure, most of his parishioners continued to attend church services and welcomed his visits to their homes.

Even the little town of Winzig did not reveal its political past with any precision. It is noteworthy, however, that no estimate of faithful Nazi followers exceeded one-third. In other words, at least two-thirds of Winzigers remained uncommitted to the Third Reich. They protected themselves with silence and conformity. The situation in the cities was, of course, different. The urban population, particularly the workers, had suffered greater deprivation in the pre-Nazi decade, and their politics sought more radical remedies than the politics of their country cousins. The Communist party had attracted millions of voters from among the discontented. Others were persuaded to join the Nazi party to seek economic and emotional relief. No wonder that the city streets became the arena for the clashes between political enemies during the early thirties.

The Nazi media created the image that Hitler led a monolithic mass movement. Undoubtedly, many Germans were enthusiastic Nazis, but careful orchestration by the Propaganda Ministry exaggerated that impression. Historians have offered their own estimates. For example, F. L. Carston asserted that Nazism never dominated the German political scene.[1] The figures suggested by Fritz Max Cahen approximate those cited for Winzig. He believed that in 1939 50 percent of the population disapproved of the course Hitler steered for the nation, 20 percent denounced his methods but not the results, and 30 percent completely endorsed Hitler's program and its execution.[2]

Had the Nazis remained in power, which is to say had they won or avoided the Second World War, Hitler's popularity would have soared. The Hitler Youth movement had enormous appeal for the children. It is likely that within a generation German Fascism would have become deeply entrenched. Most of the boys and girls enjoyed the comradery, the outings, the singing and marching by torchlight, the sense of importance and power that the youth groups injected into their training.

The problem of judging Hitler's popularity is linked to another challenge for the historian: who is guilty of the inhumanities inflicted during the twelve terrible years of Nazi rule? Are bystanders as guilty as well as perpetrators? Ought those who were unwilling instruments of crimes against humanity be separated from those who committed bestial acts voluntarily? Is a blanket condemnation of all party members or government officials unreasonably broad? The already complicated inquiry falters from the outset. What defines a Nazi? It was quite possible, for example, for a Winziger like Rektor Spieler to hate the Treaty of Versailles and support Hitler's conduct on that subject yet despise the Third Reich's abrogation of civil liberties. A conservative farmer such as Hugo Kliem favored the laws on agrarian debt alleviation but thought the anti-Semitic decrees were shameful. When the members of German professional organizations were enrolled en masse into the party, did this act make all teachers, lawyers, architects, and so forth, bonafide Nazis? There is no yardstick to measure the endless variety of circumstances that altered individual cases. The Nuremberg War Crimes Tribunals of 1945 attempted to bring to justice a few of the most notorious cases, but the problem of individual responsibility defies solution.

During the first six years of Nazi control, the routine of daily life seemed to change little in Winzig. The weather, crops, prices, the poor quality of farm labor, the disrespect of children for their elders were, as ever, the topics of concern and conversation.

Two small groups, however, did not conform to that picture: the professional Nazis and the Jews. The party leaders bought new furniture and drove official cars, and their families dressed better. They relished their power, dispensing or withholding favors through the ways of the petty bureaucracy. They chafed that no matter what title was attached to their names, the people of Winzig regarded them as usurpers. They socialized mainly with one another.

The Jews, however, at the other end of the scale, experienced a complete transformation of their lives. The process that would end with genocide began with the official identification of who is a racial Jew. The next step was the destruction of Jewish economic life. Then followed isolation, emotional and physical separation behind walls or barbed wire. Once the decision to destroy the Jews was made, the road from the ghettoes to the death camps presented no serious difficulties. But Winzig's few Jewish families had no appreciation of their danger. The idea of annihilation at the hands of a cultured, civilized nation was beyond the powers of their imagination.

Winzig's Jewish population had never consisted of more than five or six families. By 1935 two of the clothing store proprietors had sold out and retired to a larger city. The owner of the fabric shop sent his young boy to the United States and waited for his own visa somewhere other than in Winzig. Mr. and Mrs. Arnholtz, who had owned and operated a wine distillery, permitted their son and daughter to emigrate to Palestine. In 1935 they liquidated their business and followed their children. Within a few months, however, they returned. Unable to adapt to the harshness of pioneer life, they expected to live quietly in Winzig on their life's savings. They were a popular couple and in 1935 still had many loyal friends. Even in their worst nightmares they could not envision the realities of a Nazi death camp.

The Jewish Steinhardt and Moses families lived on the Vorstadt in a large complex consisting of living quarters, flour mill, bakery, barns, and gardens. They were closely related: a sister and brother had married a brother and sister. Both families had come from the province of Posen in 1920, when the Treaty of Versailles awarded that territory to Poland. The men had served in the German army. Their language and culture was German, and like many others, they established new homes within German borders. During the mid-thirties, a widowed sister and an older brother and his wife had joined the household. Food, shelter, and warmth were always abundant in that sprawling house. In the cities, most Jews had been driven from their employment and Jew baiting had become a common street sport. The notion that such terrible abuses could take place in Winzig seemed completely farfetched.

Eventually, even Winzig could not escape the violence of the Holocaust. During the war, probably in 1944, the Arnholtzes and three members of the Moses/Steinhardt family were murdered, probably at Auschwitz. Surely the people of Winzig must have known of their fate. After all, the town was little more than a village. Everyone shopped in the same few stores, drank in the same few inns, and delivered milk to the same creamery. It seemed unreasonable to believe that five people could disappear from Winzig without public knowledge. But reasonable assumptions cannot substitute for the truth. A reunion of Winzigers in West Germany in 1967 was attended by one of the Jewish immigrants to the United States. She was greeted with speeches and flowers and many inquiries about the members of her family. Questions concerning the rest of the Jewish community of Winzig were asked: "Where are your aunts and uncle? Mr. and Mrs. Arnholtz? Did they go to America or Palestine?" The visitor replied: "No, they were killed in the gas chambers!"

Shocked silence. Several men and woman murmured apologies, perhaps for asking, perhaps for the deaths; others turned away to deal with whatever emotion this news aroused. Obviously, they would not have raised the question had there been any inkling that Winzig also contributed to the statistics of the Holocaust.

On the second day of the reunion some of the Winzigers approached the American guest to justify themselves: "We knew that the Jews had been moved from their homes in town to a little hut, really a shed, in the woods. Sometimes we saw them. They were working for the forester, chopping trees and gathering wood. And then we just didn't see them anymore. We thought they left, resettled, you know. It was during the war and we all had such terrible troubles and . . ."

Anti-Semitism in a small town could not operate with the anonymity possible in cities. Here each new law affected real people with familiar faces. Almost every day Winzigers had to make choices. When Dr. Loele continued to greet and some-times stop to chat for a moment with Frau Moses, he was declaring his opposition to the regime. When Fraeulein Petzold passed Anna with a vacant stare, her position was equally clear. Urban, the policeman, crossed to the opposite side of the street as Anna approached. He hoped to offend no one, but in fact, his gesture exasperated everyone. Hugo Kliem never stopped visiting his Jewish friends, day or night. He didn't care. The master baker, Schilk, refused for as long as he could the official demand to oust the Arnholzes from the apartment he rented them. Their son Herbert showed kindness to Rita Steinhardt when no other Gentile child in town would speak to her. He taught her to play chess in the Arnholz's living room. Such was the variety of responses to Nazi intimidation.

How did the Jews of Winzig react to the changes in their lives? What were their expectations and reactions? These were families who felt comfortable with assimilation but had never considered the possibility of renouncing their faith. Their religion was an integral part of their home life. They viewed themselves as Germans of the Jewish faith. There was no conflict between these loyalties. The violent anti-Semitism of Nazi rhetoric came as a disturbing blow. How was it possible for Germans to regress from modern enlightenment to such medieval bigotry? There was concern but, in the early thirties, little fear. The vitriolic speeches of Nazi candidates for election were viewed as demagoguery. Politicians were forever seeking votes by appealing to the lowest denominators among the voters. The verbal violence was surely never to be matched by deeds.

The wisdom of the coffee Klatches had proclaimed that after the election was over this disgraceful, atavistic anti-Semitism would disappear. Was it not clear that the efforts and intelligence of all Germans would be needed to solve the nation's grave problems? To exclude Jews from this work was irrational and therefore inconceivable. Very few Germans, and surely no one in Winzig, foresaw that Nazism was about to elevate irrationality to the new national creed. For several years after Hitler became chancellor, the government exerted pressure to persuade the Jews to emigrate. Even though anti-Jewish economic restrictions accompanied this push, only the wisest among the German Jews realized the gravity of the danger. Winzig's Jews were not among the wise. In fact, news that certain relatives or acquaintances were leaving was met with raised eyebrows. Were such drastic measures really necessary? Surely the German people would soon take full measure of Hitler and oust him from power. With fortitude and patience, this storm could be weathered, as Jews had done so often in their history.

As the tempo of oppression increased, consideration was given to sending the older children out of the country. Deprived of their opportunities to enter professions or even to be trained in business, the young people had no future in Germany. Some found temporary havens in several European countries. The situation for their parents, however, grew more dangerous. When the Germans decreed that the emigrants could take nothing of value, the trickle of entrance visas to other countries all but dried up. Winzig's Jews, in their "sit tight, hold on, do not panic" posture, were representative of a large proportion of German Jews. Not until November of 1938, when the government directed a pogrom known as Krystallnacht, did they understand their peril. By then, of course, the rest of the world had closed its doors to the impoverished victims. Among the 6 million killed, more than 120,000 were German Jews, representing all but a few hundred of those unable to flee before the outbreak of the war.   In retrospect, the inability of so many German Jews to understand their peril is difficult to comprehend. As propaganda was translated into decree, step-by-step, month after month, the plan for genocide should have become clear. The rationale to shut out the truth, to deny reality until it could be denied no longer, was often unconscious. Most German Jews were intensely nationalistic. They had gained citizenship about a century earlier, granted first by the states and, after unification in 1871, by the national government. They had achieved much, in business, the professions, even the civil service. As they looked east to Poland and Russia they saw Jewish suffering, gratitude, and patriotism intertwined. Conversions to Christianity and mixed marriages had been increasing. The Jewish Reform movement originated here, and its followers viewed Judaism as a religion that could survive in the Diaspora. In 1933 the 525,000 German Jews constituted less than 1 percent of the total population. More than half of that number were self-employed and/or provided work for others. Their participation in the nation's economic life was apportioned as follows:

in commerce	3.3%
in law	8.1%
in medicine	7.1%
others	2.3%[3]

According to the endless reams of material emanating from Dr. Goebbels's propaganda machine, Jews were slumlords, pawnbrokers and moneylenders. The big lie, repeated often enough, needed no connection to the truth to be accepted by millions. We cannot know how many Germans actually believed that Jews were both extremely dangerous and subhuman. It is clear, however, that few voices, and fewer hands, were raised to protest the degradation of their fellow Jewish citizens. Hitler's admonition "the Jews are our misfortune" fell upon ground well prepared by a thousand years of hatred. The status granted Jews in modern Germany had covered up but had not destroyed deep, often unconscious, levels of anti-Semitism. Hitler created the climate to foster its regeneration. The reaction of the Christian public left no doubt that the constitutional, legal concessions of the past century had not uprooted anti-Semitism from its emotional, irrational bases.

April 1, 1933, was designated as Action Day by the NSDAP, a day of "counteroffensive against the crimes committed by International Jewry." A boycott of all Jewish business establishments was to be enforced by the public at large. In Winzig the tailor Cebulla, head of the SA, outdid himself. First, his squad spent the preceding night with tar brush and bucket painting the word "JEW" on the windows and walls of the six Jewish establishments. On the steps of the Steinhardt bakery he added: "THOSE WHO EAT JEWS' BREAD — DIE!" Similar threats appeared in front of the other stores. To enforce the boycott and for dramatic effect as well, uniformed SA troopers were posted at the entrances of the Jewish-owned shops.

The reaction of the early shoppers was one of surprise, followed by indignation. Never mind the fancy uniforms: these louts had no right to interfere with the business affairs of decent people. Employees were particularly upset. Was the SA going to pay them the day's lost wages? Several who tried to push by the sentries were blocked from entering. Since only four guards had been sent to cover the several gates to the Steinhardt/Moses establishment, some of the workers slipped in through the garden. But there was little to do; no grain was milled, no seeds or fertilizer sold, and there were no customers for the baked goods.

Except for Hugo Kliem, the boycott might have passed without incident. Kliem would not give up his daily visit to the Steinhardts. The sight of the SA infuriated him. Instead of entering the house without attracting attention-his garden adjoined Heymann's-he faced the troopers and berated them vehemently. In his rich Silesian dialect he compared them unfavorably to a number of farm animals and proceeded toward the house. By then, the troopers were enraged. A few giggling spectators were watching this embarrassing scene. Two of the SA sentries followed Kliem and caught him on the steps. They beat him with their fists, but Hugo kept going. The SA had orders not to enter the buildings, and the men had to be content to hurl threats and curses at the closed door. Inside, a very frightened Frau Steinhardt tended to Kliem's cuts and chastised him for taking such needless risks.

Although the boycott was scheduled for a day, Lang kept Winzig's SA troopers in place for an entire year. After that, there was no business activity to deter.

Legislation heralding the expulsion of Jews from Germany's economic life followed within a week after the boycott. And the laws just kept coming. The Law for the Reestablishment of Career Civil Service resulted in the dismissal of Jews from government service. At the insistence of von Hindenburg, frontline veterans of World War I were exempt, but just for the time being.[4]

Evidence was mounting that Hitler's *Mein Kampf* was a manual for action, not a mere propaganda expedient. Decree followed decree. Jews were excluded from a growing number of professions and businesses. A quota system was introduced in schools and universities. Since only three Jewish students remained in Winzig, the law required no local enactment.

Perhaps the children would have been better off had they been forced to leave. The teacher, Mai, was eager to prove himself a dedicated Nazi. He informed the Jewish children, Siegfried and Rita Steinhardt and Margot Moses, that henceforth they must sit in the back of the classroom. They must be separated from the Aryan students lest they contaminate them. They must keep still in class and, of course, must not participate in any after-school activities. Siegfried, who was thirteen years old when Hitler came to power, became the special target of a gang of Hitler Youth. They waited for him in a little park, the Anlage, to taunt and beat him. Rektor Spieler tried to help but couldn't. In 1937 the boy's parents reluctantly sent him to a Jewish trade school in Breslau. Margot and Rita were not abused physically: rather they suffered isolation, confusion, and self-doubt. Why was it really so terrible to be Jewish? Could it be true that Jews were Germany's curse? Not their parents, surely not, but others? Most bitter of all were the blows struck by their best friend, Irene. For years the three girls had been a happy trio. Now Irene spit on the ground each time she encountered the cousins. What elaborate dreams of revenge the girls nursed. Someday they would make Irene sorry. Someday they would prove their loyalty to Germany with a marvelous, heroic deed. Someday . . .

In the fall of 1935, all Jewish children were ousted from public schools. The cousins were enrolled in an academy run by the Jewish Community Council of Breslau. They were twelve years old and had never been away from home. For all their lives they would remember the faces of their parents when they left.

The Jews of Winzig were actually better off than their counterparts in the cities. The decrees that curtailed personal freedom had little direct impact here. It was outrageous and demeaning to be classified as an outcast, a leper, but laws forbidding Jews to sit on public benches, or visit parks, museums, theaters, or sport events caused no hardship in Winzig. The curfew meant nothing since there was no place to go at night anyhow. Even when the spate of anti-Semitic legislation grew macabre, when Jews were banned from the ownership and use of telephones and radios, when they could no longer ride in public transport, when they had to deliver up their pets, even their canaries, when blind Jews were forbidden the use of their white canes, when certain articles of clothing were proscribed, it was still better to be in Winzig than in Berlin.

Only after January of 1942, when the Final Solution marked European Jewry for total destruction, did the obscurity of the hinterland fail to save the remaining German Jews. The Nuremberg Laws of September 1935 deprived Jews of their citizenship. Henceforth they were unwanted guests in Germany and the ordinary protection of their lives and property was no longer their rightful due. The definition of who was a Jew or a *Mischling* (mixed breed) had finally been agreed upon. Followers of the Jewish faith were automatically non-Aryan, regardless of racial background. Three or four Jewish grandparents classified an individual as Jewish, no matter what the religious affiliation. The offspring of a mixed marriage was defined as a *Mischling*, whose legal status teetered between that of an Aryan and a Jew. Such marriages were henceforth forbidden. The law also decreed that no woman under forty-five years of age could work in a Jewish household, a provision attributable to Hitler's sexual obsession. Poor Lene, she had worked for the Steinhardts for many years and now, age forty, she said a tearful good-bye: "If Herr Hitler only knew what nice people you are, he would never make me leave."

For most German Jews, the Nuremberg Laws were a turning point. They had to consider the possibility of emigrating. Hitler's power was unchallenged and the expectation of an anti-Nazi coup was wishful thinking. The immediate anxiety concerned the children. The Arnholtz teenagers joined Youth Aliya and left to work the land in Palestine. The first of the children from the Vorstadt to leave the country was seventeen-year-old Josef Moses. The family had relatives in the United States who provided the necessary guarantees that he would not become a public charge. His sister Ruth had graduated from a Breslau *Gymnasium* in 1934 and, not knowing what to do next, had written a letter of inquiry to the United States consulate in Berlin. She simply asked what processes must be followed to be eligible for a visa. Later, in 1938, with her young husband in the Dachau concentration camp, that letter saved the young couple. The American consul validated her 1934 request for information as an application for a visa. Without that act of kindness, she would have been at the end of a four- or five-year-long waiting list. As later events confirmed, that would have been a death sentence. In 1938 she was a bride whose husband had been arrested during the Krystallnacht pogrom, just days after their entrance papers to the United States had been granted. Ruth, appearing calmer than she felt, presented her papers to the German authorities. At this time the government harassed the Jews to leave the country; the Holocaust machinery had not yet been put into place. Max Berns, the young husband, was released, and the couple left Germany immediately. In 1939, Margot, the former *Kinderfest* queen and sister of Ruth, followed. Finally, in 1940, Anna and Jakob Moses were among the last of the German Jews to exit legally. They were part of a group that left Berlin in a sealed railroad car, travelling across defeated and occupied France to neutral Spain. There a ship for tne United States awaited them.

Walter, the oldest of the Steinhardt sons, had a narrow escape. He had been studying in Berlin, where, in 1937, he joined an anti-Nazi student group. Idealists, hotheads, socialists, communists and democrats, Jews and Gentiles, they formed a supposedly nonpolitical discussion group. But the Gestapo was not deceived. Walter was in the middle of an impassioned plea for organizing anti-Nazi resistance when the doors burst open and strangers with bulging pockets took seats in the back of the room. Without the slightest hesitation, Walter launched into a speech enthusiastically promoting artificial insemination to improve livestock. He remembered arguing the topic with his father. The meeting was adjourned without disorder. But several weeks later, Walter received a telephone call from a friend who had access to the files at Gestapo headquarters. "The card with your name has been pulled out. Probably designated *Nacht und Nebel*. Do not go home!" A member of the "discussion" group provided Walter with a student visa to England. He made his way to the north German coast and from there to England. The middle son of the Steinhardts' three boys, Josef, went to Holland. The Netherlands, under pressure from Jewish organizations that defrayed the costs, consented to give young Jews a temporary haven. The teenagers enrolled in several agricultural schools, preliminary to their anticipated exodus to Palestine. In 1940, when the Germans overran Holland, Josef joined the Dutch underground and, miraculously, he survived the war. Their father, Heymann Steinhardt, was most reluctant to leave Germany. He had a deep attachment to his land and to his marvelous three-acre garden. When Jews were no longer permitted to own land, he simply circumvented the decree. Hugo Kliem became the legal owner, a formality that changed nothing. The law failed to ban Jewish ownership of farm animals-an oversight, no doubt-which enabled Steinhardt to keep his horses, cows, and poultry. So he plowed and seeded and hoped to harvest. His wife, however, did not share this attachment to the soil. She agonized over the possibility of sending the two youngest children, Siegfried and Rita, out of the country on one of the several youth transports. Siegfried was often ill and needed special care and rest. In 1937 she decided to take matters into her own hands. She wrote to her brother in the United States and appealed to him for the necessary affidavits of support. Thus she threw the first lifesaving line across the ocean. Sooner or later, her husband would surely see that there was no future left for German Jews. Steinhardt enjoyed a considerable respect and trust among many Winzigers. The very fact that he was not abandoned by several of his friends tended to encourage his five-year delusion that he could outlast Hitler. Jews had been forbidden to engage in cattle trade, but for several years after the enactment of that law Heymann engaged in secret transactions with the owner of one of the larger estates near town. *Rittergutsbesitzer* (estate owner) Koch, Steinhardt's most valued trading partner in pre-Nazi years, owned four thousand acres of farmland, meadows, and woods. Koch continued to rely on Steinhardt for his frequent and regular need to buy and sell animals. The men had worked out an arrangement that Steinhardt described thus:

> The telephone would ring, but Koch did not give his name, only the time. I knew where to meet him. On my bicycle I quickly went to the deer park of one of his estates. He usually came on horseback. And there, in a setting that almost let you forget how bad the world had become, we talked as friends as well as business partners. Such was our relationship that Koch never saw the animals he bought, nor did he question the price I quoted. During all of 1937, we met like this nearly every week. Then one of Koch's footmen denounced him and he received a warning letter from the party. I too was becoming very frightened. For nearly a year the SA posted two men in front of our house. I was afraid of being followed, and so Koch and I decided that we must not meet again. That was a painful parting.[5]

By 1938 virtually no business activity remained. But still the Moses/Steinhardt families were not completely isolated. When members of the family were harassed on their way to town and many stores displayed signs announcing that Jews would not be served, Hugo Kliem shopped for his Jewish neighbors. Other friends visited after dark, but Kliem was ever defiant and came every afternoon to decry the state of the world. Dr. Loele was another Winziger who could not be intimidated by threats. He continued to care for his Jewish patients; even his house calls did not cease. But, obviously, the household's cheerful atmosphere of pre-Nazi years had been replaced by an air of anxiety. Without children in the house, time stretched endlessly in sterile inactivity. The women played cards in the afternoons; the men read the papers and tried to make themselves useful in Heymann's barns and garden. The day's most important event was the arrival of the mailman. Any news from the children? From the U.S. Consul? This dreary inertia came to a shocking end in November of 1938.

The propaganda attacks in the German press against the Jews reached a hysterical intensity. Despite the expulsion of virtually all Jews from the nations's economic life, they were not leaving the country fast enough. About half of the German Jews, some 350,000, remained in Germany. Most of this number were desperately trying to arrange their exodus. Where to? The world had all but shut its doors. Foreign governments willing to keep open the merest crack were deluged with applications to Hong Kong, Argentina, Cuba, and other places. Never mind the climate, the business opportunities, the language. But the Nazis wanted the fatherland to be *Judenrein* (cleansed of Jews) now, not years hence. A dramatic push would spur the Jews on to greater effort. Preparations to strike such a blow began in April 1938, when a questionnaire ordered Jews to list all their remaining assets. By the summer of that year, the government had an exact accounting of their possessions, including such personal items as jewelry, candlesticks, silverware, radios, furs and rugs.[6] To expropriate this property and dramatically impel the Jews to leave required some justification. German public opinion had to be neutralized. How fortuitous that a Jew provided the Nazis with the alibi for the *Aktion* known as "the Night of the Broken Glass" — Krystallnacht.

On November 7, 1938, a confused seventeen-year-old boy named Herschel Grynzpan walked into the German embassy in Paris and shot Ernst vom Rath, a minor official. Several days earlier, Herschel's family, along with thousands of other Polish

Jews living in Germany, had been forcibly ejected from Germany and dumped on the Polish border. The Poles, however, refused entry to their expelled citizens. As a result, thousands of families lived under appalling conditions in a no-man's land between the two boundaries. Herschel quite literally worried himself sick. In an explosion of rage he sought revenge against Germany. The rather pointless assassination was the result. The Nazis, led by Goebbels, quickly realized that this provided the perfect opportunity to strike against the Jews. The event could be converted into a government-sponsored pogrom. Once and for all the remaining Jews would learn what they had not grasped before: Nazi actions were true to Nazi words. Of course, the violence would be attributed to the fury of the German people seeking reprisal for international Jewish criminality.

Under the direction of the propaganda minister, agitated news bulletins interrupted the regular radio programs to unmask the latest plot of world Jewry against the German people. The killing of vom Rath was aired as the ultimate example of the Jews' eternal compulsion to destroy the Aryans. Of the motives and the youthfulness of the assassin not a word. Vom Rath, of whom nothing was known, was enshrined as the sacrificial Teuton. Throughout the nation, the SA was mobilized. The Brownshirts were handed prepared lists of Jewish-owned property, including the addresses of homes, apartments, business establishments, schools, and synagogues. The instructions varied little from place to place: burn down the houses of worship; encourage the population to participate; wreck the shops, but do not loot; don't worry about the fire departments; they will only protect Aryan property, nor be concerned about the police; they have their orders and will not interfere.

The well-organized riot had the desired effects. Some 7,500 business establishments and all synagogues, a total of 177, were laid to waste.[7] Window smashing was particularly popular; city streets sparkled with tons of broken glass, and thus the designation Krystallnacht was coined.

When Himmler realized that Goebbels had taken the initiative, he called out his Gestapo and SS. It certainly was unfair to exclude his men from the fray, and furthermore, this was the perfect opportunity to fill the concentration camps.

During the next several days the SS and Gestapo systematically arrested all German Jewish men between the ages of sixteen and sixty. The Nazis invaded homes, searched trains, and combed the streets. It was a successful effort! Within a week thirty thousand men and boys were shipped to Dachau, Buchenwald, and other concentration camps.[8]

The arrest of Max Berns, husband of the former Ruth Moses, was quite typical of the Gestapo methods. The young couple had gone to Berlin to complete the paperwork for their emigration to the United States. Frau Steinhardt, always eager to escape the boredom of Winzig, had accompanied them. The three were returning to Winzig on the very night that vom Rath died. They had no inkling of impending events until they arrived at the railroad station in Berlin. Why were people screaming? Men with truncheons were beating other men. Bloody faces, crying women, hysterical children were everywhere. Who were the men dragged away by the SS? What crimes had they committed? Why did no one help, not even the police? Many passengers, those not directly involved, stood aside, glanced quickly at the scene, and hurried away. In the general confusion, the three managed to board the train back to Silesia. With the help of a newspaper, they began to understand that they were caught in the whirlpool of a pogrom-a terrifying realization. If only they could get to Winzig. But first they must change trains in Steinau. Here too the platform was swarming with Nazi uniforms. The SS and Gestapo seemed overwhelmed by the task assigned to them. Men who resisted as well as those who submitted quietly were beaten indiscriminately. "Jew?" someone asked Max. He nodded. Several blows struck his head, but nevertheless Ruth threw herself at her husband in a display of hysteria. While the SS men cursed and tried to pull her away, Max slipped into her hand their precious emigration papers. Then he was dragged out of sight. Ruth and her Aunt Rosa held each other and cried together. But not for very long; they had to get home.

All of the Jewish men in Winzig were arrested. Not Urban but two unfamiliar SS men arrived at the house on the Vorstadt about eight in the evening. They checked off the names: Heymann Steinhardt, Adolph Steinhardt and Jakob Moses. No charges were read, but an order was issued: "Hurry up, hurry up and get into the car outside."

Heymann asked if he could change from his slippers to a pair of shoes. The Nazi replied by placing his hand on the gun in his holster. Anna Moses stood silently by as the men rushed from the house. No good-byes were exchanged; the front door slammed, and she was alone. The events of the next two days are best described by Heymann Steinhardt:

> They took us — we were four; Arnholtz was there already — to the basement of the city hall. We stood around for several hours. They wouldn't tell us anything. Finally, a police car drove up and took us to Wohlau. At the police station we were searched. "If any weapons are found," the SS man said, "you will be shot to death instantly." We were put into a cell and told to undress. We were very hungry, but we couldn't touch the stinking potato and dried up herring that were thrown at us. In the morning, a car took us to Breslau. The guards pushed and shoved us, but we were not seriously hurt. Breslau looked like a battlefield. Many synagogues were burning. So much broken glass and merchandise in the street. Police cars and fire trucks were everywhere. We were taken to the central police headquarters, not into the building but into the exercise yard. Some of us were beaten with clubs when we got out of the car. I was lucky, just a graze. There were thousands of men in the yard. Just milling around. So quiet. An unbelievable sight. No guards among the prisoners, just in the towers and the walk atop the wall. We stayed like that all day. Cold, hungry, and scared. We talked very little. No one really knew anything. Everyone worried about his family and looked for relatives or friends. Suddenly I realized that I had become separated from the other Winzigers. That was the worst moment. Toward evening the Gestapo and SS ordered us to form lines in front of the many doors to the building. The prisoners went in, but none came out.
>
> It was cold, and I had a lot of trouble because of the slippers. Especially after sundown. I was sure that the tingling in my toes meant frostbite. What good

would I be to anyone without feet? So I stepped out of my line and walked through a small wooden door I had noticed earlier. It led to something like a boiler room. It was dark and no one was there. At first, I just wanted to sit down and warm my feet. Then I had an idea. At least let me try to get away, try to get home. So I went up some steps into a corridor. There were offices on both sides. I walked through the third door. Dozens of men at work. Police, Gestapo, SA and SS, I thought. They were questioning the prisoners, taking down names, addresses and such.

I looked around for an older official, gray-haired, not in a uniform. God, I was frightened when I walked up. "Excuse me, please, but I am a farmer. I have to take care of my animals. My cows especially. They need milking. Germany needs that milk. I respectfully request my release." The official looked up from his papers. "*Juden Schweinehund*," he shouted, "get out of here at once!"

I left, but through a door opposite the one I had used to come in. Now I was in the central corridor. It was a beehive, people rushing from place to place.

At the end of the hallway I saw an exit sign, and I quickly walked that way, fast but not too fast. I passed an SA man who was shoving and pushing an old man. "Wait!" the Nazi yelled. "Here, take this cripple with you!."

The old fellow seemed to be in great pain. He hung on to me as if he were drowning. With his head on my chest, he whispered, "Why have you been released?"

I whispered back, "I haven't. And you?"

"Unfit to travel."

I said, "I don't know what to do next."

"We'll show my pass. Maybe they won't look too closely. It's worth a try." We had reached the large entrance lobby. Sentries with rifles guarded the exit.

"Halt!", one of them shouted.

"Captain," I said, "this man is ill. One of the officers ordered me to take him home."

With that, my companion barely lifted his arm to

show his pass. I wondered if the guard could see my heart pounding like a hammer. A wave of the hand and we went through the door. Just like that. Other sentries stood outside, and one of them said, "Lucky dogs," when we got to the bottom of the steps. And then we were out in the street.

Was it possible? Were we free? As fast as possible we moved away from the police station. I felt light-headed, and it took a few minutes before I noticed how well the old man was doing. Not holding my arm. Back straight. In fact, he was stepping along like a youngster. When we stopped in a dim alley, he started to laugh. He doubled up with laughter. I just stared at him, speechless. That man was actually younger than me.

"Who are you?"

He replied, "If you went to the Jewish theater of Breslau you might know my name. But it doesn't matter. What a performance I gave tonight." And then he did a little dance right there in the street. I must have said, "Donnerwetter," ten times. I tried to thank him, but he cut me short. "Let's go home." We shook hands and that's how we parted.[9]

Heymann made his way to the apartment of a cousin who lived in Breslau. The husband had been arrested but his tearful wife made Heymann welcome. There was a rumor that telephones owned by Jews were tapped, so he did not dare to call Winzig. He ate, slept a little, and forced his feet into a pair of his cousin's shoes. On the following night he got on a train to Winzig-a nerve-racking and dangerous trip. What would he find at home? After the sights he had seen in Breslau, he feared the worst. But there was his house, solid and whole. The door was locked. He threw a handful of gravel against his bedroom window. The curtain parted and he saw three familiar faces: his wife, his sister, and his niece Ruth. Rosa collapsed running down the stairs and Anna opened the door for him. She greeted him and then looked up and down the street. Heymann understood and sadly shook his head. No, he did not know what had happened to the other men.

Steinhardt stayed indoors for several days. Then Hugo Kliem let it be known around town that Heymann had been released in order to take care of his farm animals. No one bothered to check the story.

Most of the men, including the Winzigers who were arrested on Krystallnacht, were released within several months. The complete destruction of European Jewry was not yet the Nazi design. For the moment Krystallnacht served several purposes. First, it taught the Nazis that the rest of the world did not really care about Jews, a lesson they would remember well. Second, the Nazis realized that the German Gentiles were quite willing to close their eyes to the fate of the German Jews. And finally, the pogrom was turned into an economic boon. Not only were the Jews totally and finally excluded from the German economy, but by declaring that all Jews were collectively guilty of the assassination of vom Rath, the enormous fine of 1 billion marks was levied against them. This amount impoverished the German Jewish community at the very moment that its social services were desperately needed. Furthermore, all insurance claims resulting from the rampage were payable, not to the policyholders, but to the government.

The Nazis then issued a declaration that any money or property the Jews owned had been acquired illegally. Such ill-gotten gains could not be taken from the country. Now the German Jews that were able to escape had to leave as paupers, with only 10 Marks per person. The hysterical atmosphere of the pogrom produced one anti-Semitic decree after another. Local authorities were empowered to exclude Jews from living in certain areas.[10] All items of value; gold, silver, precious stones, pearls, and works of art, had to be surrendered. Property owned by Jews was Aryanized (sold to non-Jews at bargain prices). Even then, the payments had to be transferred to banks and doled out in small monthly payments.[11] Heymann Steinhardt's property serves as a case in point. For taxation purposes it had been appraised at 100,000 marks. It was Aryanized for 30,000 marks, and the local bank allowed the family only 300 marks per month. Fortunately, the new owner was not interested in taking immediate possession and now rented the house back to its "former" owners.

Heymann Steinhardt received, at long last, an affidavit of

support from American relatives early in 1939. This document was required before applying for immigration papers to the United States. Under the U.S. National Origins Plan, a greater number of Germans were admitted than Poles. The Polish quota was filled for years in advance. For reasons best known to officials in the U.S. State Department, individuals born in the province of Posen when it was still part of Germany were nevertheless placed under the Polish quota. It is difficult indeed not to assume that anti-Semitic bias played a role in such an arbitrary ruling. In 1938 that meant a delay of three to four years, a waiting time all too often cut short by the gas chambers. But the Steinhardt family was fortunate. By merest chance they learned of a loophole, a piece of Americana left over from the Homestead Acts of the 1860s. Farmers were exempted from immigration quotas, on the theory that they would never become public charges.

The reams of paper necessary to prove the farmer status of Heymann and eighteen-year-old Siegfried had been forwarded to the U.S. Consulate in Berlin. Then a puzzling request was received. Father and son were asked to take a test at the consulate. A test? No one had any idea what to expect. On their return to Winzig they gave this description: "A member of the consulate staff called us, one at a time, into a little room. On the table was a tray that had five or six compartments, each filled with a little heap of grain: rye, oats, wheat, barley, perhaps one or two others. We were asked to name them. It took just a few seconds to identify each of the grains. The young man from the Consulate nodded, smiled and we shook hands. That was it, that was the test![12]

There was much admiration for the beautiful simplicity of the test among the Winzigers. And within just a few weeks the life-giving letter arrived from Berlin. The visas would be granted, to be stamped into the passports upon their presentation. Ordinarily, the issuance of passports was a routine matter. But not for the Steinhardts. Nollenberg, the town clerk, Mayor Lang, and his alter ego, Schaube, amused themselves with a cruel game. Every week Heymann appeared, hat in hand, at the town hall to request the passports. Each time he was given a bland smile and told to come back. When he protested, he was threatened. Several times during the ensuing months, an embarrassed Urban came to arrest Steinhardt on obviously contrived charges: a window had not been darkened completely as required by the nightly black-outs, the dog had barked and neighbors complained, and so forth. Usually, after a night in the cell in the basement of the *Rathaus*, he was released. Once he was kept for several days. Since Winzig had no provisions for feeding prisoners, his wife packed meals for him. Rita felt very important when she brought soup and bread to her father in his tiny room with the barred window. She sat on the cot while he ate and laughed at his stories about two clever flies, he named them Max and Moritz, that kept him company.

The summer came and endless columns of mobile military units passed through Winzig from the west toward the Polish border. The propaganda machine accused the Poles of acts of brutal aggression against their German minority. The nation was being prepared for war. Only once did the people of Winzig greet the passing soldiers, when a hometown boy passed through town. No jubilation, no flowers or cheers welcomed the prospect of war. The memories of 1918 had not yet healed, and September 1, the start of World War II, passed in silence. And still the four Steinhardts had no passports.

In early December a letter from the U.S. consulate prompted dismay as well as action. The consul advised that if the visas were not utilized within a matter of weeks they would become invalid. Heymann decided he must explain the reasons for the delay directly to the consul. He packed a suitcase with food already scarce in ration-plagued Germany: butter, eggs, a duck, and a fat goose. He had no doubt these items would pave the way to an immediate, unscheduled appointment. Indeed, the consul general was persuaded to give Steinhardt a few minutes. He listened to the story with increasing anger. Obviously, petty egomania was preventing the rescue of a family. He called for his secretary and dictated the following telegram to Mayor Lang:

> It has come to my attention that you are opposing the announced policy of your government by withholding passports from the family of H. Steinhardt. Local authorities are expected to facilitate, not impede, the

emigration of German Jews. If the passports are not issued at once I will feel obligated to report this irregularity to the appropriate office in Berlin.[13]

On the following day Heymann received the passports. Lang, Schaube, and Nollenberg were nowhere to be seen. Within two weeks the family's American passage was booked on a Dutch ship. The good-byes were tearful as old friends came to the house after dark. But most wrenching was parting with the relatives, whose future was dreadfully uncertain.

Hugo Kliem insisted on taking the family to the train depot. As he urged his horses on, great tears streamed down his white beard. He wanted to kiss his friends on the station platform, but Rosa reminded him, "That's *Rassenschande* [a racial crime]. Someone may be watching. Just let us go, old friend; let us go."

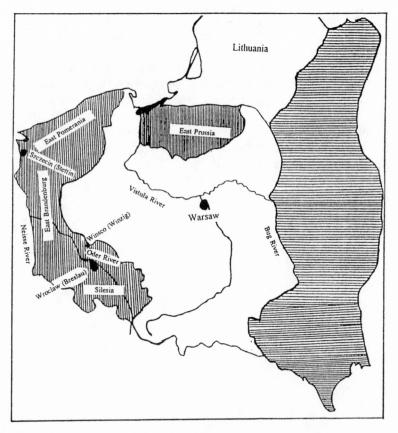

Poland, Territorial Changes in 1939-1945

Horizontally lined area: Polish territory ceded to the Soviet Union in 1939.
Vertically lined area: German territory ceded to Poland in 1945.

5

The Death of Winzig

Germany's declaration of war against Poland was accepted in Winzig with neither surprise nor enthusiasm. Mobile units of the army had rolled through the town since the late summer of 1939, and the Propaganda Ministry had tried in vain to stir up some patriotic passion. For several months preparations for the prospect of war had been in progress. Ration books for food, gasoline, and other essentials had been distributed, and blackout drills were practiced routinely. The entire economy was geared up for war production, and finally, the armed forces were placed on alert.

Most of the Silesian people were nervous about the chances of a Polish breakthrough. The Polish border, after all, was not more than an hour or two away. Was a breakthrough by the Polish army a possibility? No one dared to voice this fear in public. When victory over Poland was achieved within a mere three weeks of fighting, the people of Winzig shared in a general sigh of relief. But even then there was no jubilation. The declaration of war by France and England spoiled the hopes of a "little war," and like families everywhere, Winzigers dreaded the predictable slaughter.

One of Winzig's own, the oldest of the Scholz boys, had served in the army in the Warsaw area. When he came home on leave, he presented his mother with a sewing machine and a fur coat that was almost, but not quite, spoiled by a bullet hole in the back. Neighbors came to admire such fine gifts and tried to hide their envy. It would be no problem at all to sew up that little puncture.

The great victories of 1940, culminating in the defeat of France, though thrilling and gratifying, could not appease the disquieting remembrances of World War I. Hadn't their armies then won many great battles and in the end lost the war? There could be no rejoicing until the nation was at peace and the soldiers were home once again. In the meantime, there was much work for everyone, because only the best of everything was good enough for the men at the front.

Winzigers, like most Germans, experienced no great privations until the winter of 1943-44. During the first four years after the fall of Poland, there were personal tragedies, of course. Sons and husbands were killed, and there was great weariness, sometimes exhaustion, as the demands upon the civilian population grew ever more burdensome. However, the rhythm of life on the land remained basically unaltered. Unlike the victims of the countries they conquered, the German people experienced no brutalization, no starvation, no enslavement. Until the bombing raids of the Allies brought death and terror to the cities, life was tolerable, even though the hours of work were stretched to the limit and sometimes beyond. On the farms, children and the elderly lost the luxury of play and rest and women were more visible in the fields. In their clumsy shoes and full skirts, their hair tied back with cotton kerchiefs, they plowed and reaped like men. During 1943 foreigners, more precisely slave laborers, from the subjugated nations began to arrive in the region. Notwithstanding international law, some prisoners of war were also pressed into service to support the German war economy.[1] Polish, Soviet, and French workers were distributed among the shorthanded farmers and large estate owners. It is safe to assume that, for the most part, these unwilling "guests" of the Reich had a better chance to survive than the families they left behind. They ate and slept in quarters provided by their employers, for very little or no payment at all. Individual treatment varied from generous to contemptible, according to the disposition of their masters. In the absence of any young or even middle-aged German men, rumors were rife that some of Winzig's maidens found some of the foreigners quite appealing.

Allied air raids caused another change in the life of a small Silesian towns and villages. The increased frequency and intensity of the bombings of larger cities produced a major population shift. Women and children were evacuated from urban centers to rural areas. Silesia was considered a particularly safe haven. Between 1939 and 1943 its population increased by 232,000.[2] In addition to strangers sent by government-organized transports, relatives and friends of Winzigers sought refuge from aerial attacks in many small towns. Every spare room in hotels and private homes was occupied by new faces. The hospital, too, was enlisted for special duty. As Breslau's medical facilities were overstrained with war wounded, long-care patients were distributed in the countryside. For example, the Catholic nursing sisters of Winzig's hospital were assigned some forty patients suffering from tuberculosis.

The presumption that the eastern region of the nation was secure ended abruptly with the Soviet counteroffensive of 1944. Suddenly the distance to the eastern front was shrinking with every news bulletin. Even the most sanguine observers saw that the westerly progression of the Red armies was aimed at the Reich itself and that German arms were unable to stem their advance. More than ever, Joseph Goebbels's assurances of German invincibility had a hollow ring. The entire military situation was failing in the east and the west. The seams of the Thousand-Year Reich were splitting open. Italy fell, Normandy was invaded, and air attacks became routine. Defeat, a word the Germans had reserved for other people, was rediscovered in silence and in fear. When the specter of military collapse loomed as a distinct possibility, an attempt was made on Hitler's life. On July 20, 1944, a small faction of army officers, in association with several civilians, tried and failed to assassinate Hitler. The fuehrer, who had become a half-mad caricature of his former self, nevertheless was still capable of unleashing his fury. One hundred and fifty officers were executed immediately, and when his killers had completed their hunt, several thousand Germans were murdered, often by cruel, even bizarre methods.[3] The miscarriage of the plot aborted the hope for an immediate armistice. The war would go on until total defeat.

The eagerness of the Gestapo and SS to carry out Hitler's orders and assassinate such men as the renowned General Rommel confirmed the weakness of the anti-Nazis. Today's

Germans have elevated the plot to be a symbol of protest against the Nazis. It is depressingly true, however, that the German people failed to use this opportunity to overthrow the regime. The destruction would continue into the very heart of Berlin. And it is also true that the conspiracy was a result of Hitler's mismanagement of the war rather then revulsion with the atrocities committed by Germans throughout the length and breadth of Europe. So the plotters and many who had no part in the scheme, were hung from meat hooks with piano wires. But the German people did not rise up. Not then, not ever! Even in defeat, the Nazis could still count on obedience from the very people they had so shamefully and shamelessly betrayed.

The debacle of July 20 underlined the grim consequences of waging war against the Nazis from within. A number of elements combined to prevent the conversion of anti-Nazi conviction into successful anti-Nazi action. Fear, of course, played the primary role and the events following July 20 confirmed the legitimacy of that fear. In 1944, after four years of war, physical and mental exhaustion were also taking a heavy toll; people just hoped to get through another day. Deeply rooted ideals of loyalty, obedience, and patriotism incapacitated others. The fanatical loyalty to Hitler of men who would lose everything if Hitler fell paralyzed opposition from within the Nazi hierarchy. There simply was no one except Hitler to command the center of the stage.

As Allied military forces pushed toward the German center from east and west, Goebbels, Hitler's ever-faithful slave, was promoted. His newest and final designation was that of "Pleni-potentiary for the Winning of the War." With that title came great power. The entire Nazi party machinery was at his disposal to attempt to stop or impede the Allied invasion forces once they were on German soil. Critical decisions concerning production, distribution, and allocation of materials were now within his prerogative. He had become a warlord whose domain theoretically exceeded, and actually often conflicted with, military determinations.[4] Goebbels gave the *Gauleiters*, ad-ministrative party hacks, the power to determine when civilians in their districts could be evacuated to escape the invading armies of the Allies. These men were politicians who based their decisions on falsely optimistic propaganda rather than military or humanitarian considerations. In the final weeks of the war, the fate of hundreds of thousands of Germans would be in their generally inept hands, adding immeasurably to the misery of the people caught between two opposing armies.[5]

The German forces were unable to halt the advancing Soviets. In an act of desperation, Goebbels called out the Volkssturm. Men between the ages of sixteen and sixty-five who were not already in uniform were mobilized into this paramilitary service. Exemptions granted earlier were revoked, nor were disabilities allowed to disqualify anyone.[6] The party, through its civilian *Gauleiters*, controlled the Volkssturm. Some of these units of boys, older men, and the physically impaired, were commanded by SS officers, and a few were attached to retreating army units. Goebbels declared that these defenders constituted a human wall that would protect the frontiers. In Silesia, several components of this human wall served with General Glaeser's Fourth Panzer Army. Other units were ordered to dig ditches, presumably to prevent General Konev's First Ukrainian Army from breaking through.[7] The directive to remove the remaining men from the civilian population for such absurd work seems, at first glance, a pathetic gesture, but on further consideration this was a particularly cruel blow. At the very time that the evacuation of the region was imminent, women and children were deprived of the moral and physical support of men.[8]

The front moved inexorably closer to Winzig as 1944 neared its conclusion. The Soviet offensive stabilized temporarily along the Vistula River in mid-October. From this region the Nazis had forcibly ejected many thousands of Polish landowners, settling German families in their place. Now these Germans were put to flight, seeking refuge within the boundaries of the old Reich. As they streamed westward, they described their terrifying encounters with Soviet troops. For years Nazi propaganda had promoted dread of the "uncivilized hordes" from the East. But this was different: these were actual victims reciting in agonizing detail murders, rapes, arson and the roundup of the able-bodied for slave labor. As groups of fleeing women and children passed through eastern Germany, fear intensified for the Germans awaiting permission to escape from the path of the invaders. Unless and until the *Gauleiter* issued the decree of evacuation, they were trapped.

Despite the clear and shocking evidence that Soviet troops were hammering at the gates of the nation, it was a crime to speak of, or prepare for, flight. Instead of planning for the obvious, the *Gauleiters* still clung to the unrealistic promises of their leaders. Events in Gau Wartheland in western Poland·were a prologue for the disaster to come. That *Gauleiter's* fear of offending his Nazi superiors caused 674,000 Germans to be caught in the middle of the fighting. The civilians in the area were ground between the German and Soviet armies, and thousands of people died needlessly.[9]

The myth that the fatherland was inviolate died hard. Wishful thinking kept alive the expectation that the fuehrer would, at any moment, unveil the secret weapon that would end the war. Reports of serious contention among the Allies cropped up from time to time and fanned a glimmer of hope for an early peace. Even the notion that the total exhaustion of men and material on all sides would bring an end to the slaughter found disciples. Surely, so folk wisdom asserted, the fighting would stop before it reached German soil, just as it had during World War I. Only in nightmares did the possibility of invasion take form.

The town of Winzig was located on the east side of the Oder. It was a generally accepted understanding that if the unthinkable happened, then the Oder River would serve as the last fixed barrier against Soviet troops. What, then, was to be the fate of the German population on the east side of the Oder? Because the mere raising of such a question was treasonable and because the government maintained its policy of deceptive platitudes, no solution was offered.

The Soviet offensive crossed into Germany in January 1945. By the end of the month, all the territory east of the Oder was captured, with little German opposition. General Zhukov crossed the Oder with 180 divisions during his thrust toward Berlin. General Konev, to Zhukov's south, advanced into Silesia.[10] The Oder bridgehead at Steinau, a few miles from Winzig, was in Soviet hands on the twenty-third. The German High Command ordered the destruction of the bridge, but General Nehring's Twenty-fourth Panzer Corps and von

Sauken's Grossdeutschland Army were unable to retake the position. With the exception of the fierce battle for Breslau, the only significant struggle between the German and Soviet forces in this sector took place in Steinau.[11] The great expectations of Nehring's army, his so-called *wandernde Kessel*, or movable fortress, remained unfulfilled. His was a paper army composed of remnants and survivors of other decimated or exhausted units. Even when Nehring was reinforced by von Sauken, he was unable to carry out his orders to stem the Soviets at Glogau. His momentary resistance at a site not far from Winzig changed nothing in the overall history of the war.[12] While German soldiers, still obedient to their officers, were vainly trying to follow impossible commands, conditions for noncombatants were deteriorating rapidly.

The winter of 1944-45 was an exceptionally cold one. Refugees from the combat zones struggled westward amid bullets from friend and foe. Snow and ice and contradictory official directives compounded their trauma. The anguish that the Nazis had visited upon millions of Europeans had turned like a boomerang to strike at German faces, but they were the faces of the old, of women and children. Streams of refugees pushed west in horse-drawn wagons, loaded with a few treasured belongings and the all- important bales of hay. The able-bodied walked to ease the burden for the horses because the death of a horse would often forecast the death of the owner.

Father Willinek, Winzig's Catholic priest, left us a picture of Winzig during those weeks:

> Never to be forgotten is the image of the endless flow of the dispossessed from the eastern provinces. They entered Winzig from Herrnstaedter Street, their caravans almost silent in the thick snow as they moved toward the Ring. Then their trek to they knew not where turned into Wohlauer Vorstadt, winding its way to Steinauer Strasse, toward the Oder and its bridges. Alas, these refugees often found a momentary happy respite in the deserted homes of our townspeople who had moved northward on Saturday or Sunday. For a few hours their houses came to life. Stoves were lit, food

that had been left behind was cooked, and the homeless
children found toys that gave them a temporary illusion
of safety.

For how long would these wanderers keep the
goods they carried in their wagons?

. . . As their draft horses tired, items were pulled off
and ended up in the ditches along the road.[13]

The fighting front was mere hours away, and still the order
to evacuate was not given. *Gauleiter* Karl Hanke of Lower
Silesia was still trying to prove his faith in the fuehrer by
refusing to organize, or even to permit, an orderly withdrawal
of the population. The brief hope that the "magical" General
Schoerner could provide the miracle of holding back the Red
Army had no substance. The plan to make a stand along the
Oder disintegrated, and by the end of January all of Silesia was
in Soviet hands. General Konev crossed the river and pushed
north and west toward Berlin. Silesia's civilians were among
the approximately 5 million Germans left to fend for
themselves as the Soviet forces advanced.

German scholars have amassed volumes of documents on
their fate. Among these records, the fate of the people from
Winzig is but a single note in a mournful chorus. The figures
listed below are admittedly approximations, due to the chaotic
conditions of the flight:

German population of Silesia at the beginning of 1945	4,700,000
Remained behind or overtaken along the way	1,500,000
Fled to Czechoslovakia	1,600,000
Fled to Reich territory: Saxony, Thuringia, Bavaria	1,600,000[14]

Fugitives from Silesia had better chances of escaping the
war zone than their counterparts from the northern regions of
eastern Germany. The Silesian-Czech border remained open,
while Pomeranians, East Prussians, and West Prussians found
their routes toward the center of the Reich blocked by the
Soviet armies. Winzigers, like most refugees from Middle and

Upper Silesia, trekked south into the Sudetenland. Although the Czechs could hardly be expected to welcome them with open arms, the area accorded them relative safety.

Eastern Silesians, that is, Silesians living on the east side of the Oder, totaled approximately 700,000 people. Of that number, about 600,000 were in flight during a four or five day period in January of 1945. Although the most terrifying danger, entrapment in the midst of battle, was not commonly encountered by these groups, the flight was a test of physical and emotional endurance. Several factors combined to challenge even the most intrepid of the refugees:

1. The winter of 1945 was a particularly harsh one.
2. Political expedience delayed the proclamation of evacuation orders; in some cases such orders were never issued.
3. Transportation facilities, particularly trains, were unable to handle the numbers clamoring for service.
4. The absence of men placed extraordinary burdens on the women.
5. The general confusion was further compromised by the lack, or inadequacy, of official instructions.[15]

A typical directive to evacuate read as follows:

Attention!   Fellow Citizens! The situation makes it necessary to depart. The population has two choices of transportation. Citizens can use their own vehicles or use the special trains that will leave at specified intervals. The first train is for mothers and their children under six years old; the next train is for pregnant women and the seriously wounded war casualties. Next the elderly and their companions may leave. Following that a special train for mothers with older children will be provided. Lastly, all others except members of the Volkssturm, that is, males between the ages of sixteen and sixty, may depart.

What to take: the minimum of necessities weighing not more than twenty-five kilos excluding bedding. Take eating utensils and warm clothing. Children must

wear name tags for identification. Remain quiet and
orderly and help one another.[16]

The most cursory examination of the order revealed its
flaws. What mother would be separated from her children?
What was the destination of the various trains? Who qualified
as a companion for an elderly person? Would there be food,
shelter and medical care during and at the end of the journey?
Railroad tracks as well as the stations were frequently under
enemy attack; therefore, only those who had no other means of
transport trusted their lives to the trains. But most tragic was
the fact that very few trains were still running. Most people
assembled at designated points and waited in vain.

Winzig's farmers owned horses and wagons, and for the
most part they followed the general regional pattern of heading
west and south. Those without their own means of transportation had no choice but to try their luck with the railroad.
Cars were useless. There was no gasoline for private citizens.

In later years a number of townspeople recorded the
experiences of their flight for a small publication, called
Heimatklaenge, a newsletter by and for Winzigers in exile.
Father Willinek led the effort to give a sense of continuity to
his former congregation and their neighbors through his
"Sounds from Home." Its pages provided an outlet for a
common sense of loss and gave voice to the dream to return
to the good old years of the past. Friends who were separated
since the flight found one another and shared their memories.
Two individual histories concerning the escape from Winzig
first published in the *Heimatklaenge* are offered here. The first
article was written by Father Willinek, the second one by
Elfriede Matschke, the wife of a farmer near the Vorstadt.
Their stories are representative of the fate of hundreds of
thousands of Silesians during the last days of January 1945.

Father Willinek's last day in Winzig was indeed harrowing.
What solace could he offer his distraught parishioners? No one
knew what lay ahead. And yet, he was more fortunate than
thousands of others who also had no private means of transportation and were forced to escape on foot. When it was obvious
that the government could not provide transport, these unfor-
tunates, with their children and a few possessions in their arms,

streamed westward in the snow of mid-winter.

The father described his departure as follows:

I was at breakfast with members of my family on Saturday, January 20, 1945, when the merchant Franz Heinse entered. With obvious excitement he reported that the immediate evacuation of women and children had been ordered. The news was like a thunderbolt. By a twist of the hand of fate our accustomed way of life, our usual order, our whole culture was ended. Even though we had been burdened with the war and had feared for our safety under the Nazis, there was still meaning to our lives. With a minimum of time we were ordered to look through our possessions and select the few things of value to be taken along. Each family had to part with many things that normally enrich one's life.

The order to leave suddenly changed the relationship between worker and employer. No master could assume responsibility for his workers anymore. Farmers could not continue to care for the livestock in their barns. Fortunate indeed were the employers who could count on aid and advice from their workers and share with them the expulsion. The true meaning of evacuation was, after all, expulsion. How strange! About eight days before the evacuation order was issued, a master baker in our vicinity was arrested because he advised someone to pack his bags. He was charged with defeatism. It was also interesting that several of the big shots had already disappeared with bag and baggage before the ordinary citizen was permitted to leave. It had been carefully explained to me by the mayor (Lang) that I too must leave when the town administrators depart. Only the Volkssturm was to remain behind. During the night of January 23, however, when my sister and I went to the train, I saw no Volkssturm. What we did find were hundreds of fellow sufferers and a single railroad employee. We all followed with great anxiety his hours of pleading with the authorities to finally secure a train. No doubt that man was responsible for getting us out of town. Oh, my, what promises had been made by the Nazis during the last three days.

For example:

Those still in Winzig on January 22 should assemble at the Ring. Army transport would remove everyone. No transport came, not even for the hospital and its women and girls suffering from lung diseases. In the evening an army vehicle finally arrived for the bedridden patients. They were taken to Lueben, where their particular fate was sealed and they were forever free of concern over their future. [According to Father Willinek, the patients were set upon the ground in a field and then shot to death].

We were told that Silesia would not be given up by the army, not even the right bank of the Oder River. In fourteen days we would all be permitted to return. Our evacuation was a temporary military necessity; that is what I was told at the town hall on January 21. . .

Those were turbulent days. The ever-increasing demands made on me were sometimes too much for me; I freely make that admission.

To those who today criticize, sometimes vociferously, the action of the people, to them I can only say: If you were not in a position of responsibility toward others and yourself, if you were not called upon to make hurried decisions, then you cannot sit in judgment today without being suspected of hypocrisy. Even historians will do well not to make judgments except in the light of the circumstances of that time.

Several of our fellow sufferers in Winzig managed to evade the order to leave. These were mainly elderly people who did not believe themselves well enough to withstand the hardships of flight. Perhaps they were confident that their politically pure hearts would earn them mercy at the hands of the victors. They gambled for high stakes, health, safety, life itself.

I do not know how many of those who remained

behind survived the onslaught. But I do know that in those January days the following suffered a quick though painful death: Mr. Schoepe and daughter, Miss Zapke, Mr. Danke, the two sisters Polaski, Dr. Loele, his wife and their housekeeper. The list is incomplete. It does not include the many who died during the flight, nor those who perished in the final exodus ordered by the Poles.[17]

The Winzigers who had milled about the open railroad platform were able to board the train secured by that single heroic railway employee. They headed west, first stopping in Liegnitz, then progressing deeper into central and western Germany. Most of the families who fled by train remained in the same general area. The last stop of the train was a new beginning for many Silesians. There, however, they were outsiders, intruders in the towns and villages of their resettlement. The local western Germans accepted them with a full gamut of responses, from outright hostility to sympathetic understanding. But they survived.

The fate of many of Winzig's farmers took a very different turn. Since they owned horses and wagons, they generally opted to flee with their teams, individually or in small groups. The wagon made it possible to take essential but bulky items such as featherbeds, pots, and pans and perhaps some family treasures. The intent and hope of these trekkers was, first, to get out of the battle area. Second, since the initial wave of Soviet soldiers would surely vent their fury on the German population, it would be best to await events in Czechoslovakia. Finally, when some sort of provisional government was in place, they would return. They hoped the horses would survive and they would be back in time for the spring plowing. Perhaps even some of the livestock they released into the woods might pull through.

Elfriede Matschke was one of the thousands of women who had to make the fateful decisions of that last January of the war. The men in the family had been claimed by the government. Her farm was just outside of Winzig in the hamlet of Froeschen. She described her ordeal as follows:

On January 23 at noon my dear mother and I were the last to leave Froeschen. I drove through Brunnwiese, Krischwitz, from there to Wischitetz, Krehlau, and on to Steinau. There I crossed the Oder. By then it was evening and I did not know which way to turn. Where could I go? I decided to go to Lampersdorf. . . .
There we spent the night in a cow barn. On the 24th of January we moved on through Parchwitz toward Liegnitz. . . We stayed there until February 7. The Russians were approaching. We moved on toward Kossendau, where we remained until the 11. But there we had to hurry; the Russians were shooting over our heads. On to Goldberg and heading for Neukirch.

We were now encountering our first mountains. My wagon had no brakes at all. That caused a dangerous situation. We arrived in Neukirch in the evening and spent a terrifying night.

On February 12 it was rumored that the Russians were about to arrive. Here, in Neukirch, we tended our first wounded. We moved on at four in the afternoon. The German army was always alongside on the road, overtaking us. At nightfall, in Rosenau, it was again said that the Russians were on the way. Next morning, despite the snow, we pushed on until we reached Schoenau and the Hohenliebenthal. We remained there until the 5, but we were refused provisions. We moved on again, through the Johannes Valley and over the Kappellen Mountain. All without brakes. Dreadful, it was dreadful!

When we arrived in Berbelsdorf my horse became very ill. Some of our soldiers were very helpful. The roads had become very icy. We stayed until the 12 of March and then moved on to Herischdorf. We stayed for two days but were quartered in two different places in that brief time. We always slept in the wagon. Our journey now proceeded to Voigsdorf. There I was called to stand horse muster.[18]

One of the horses kicked my hand. My injury was quite severe. But fortunately I was allowed to keep my horse. And that was very, very important. My bay mare

was, however, still ailing. I treated her every day as
best I could without medication. While in Voigsdorf,
I had to report for work on the defense bulwarks in
order to get feed for my horse. In the morning I
worked alone, in the afternoon I had to report with my
horse.

We stayed in this town until the armistice. That day
we fled, but the Russians sent us "home." That meant
Voigsdorf. The events of that day cannot be described.
I could never live through another day like it.[19]

Elfriede had been in flight for over three months. She had
no difficulty recording, in her matter-of-fact style, the details of
her ordeal, all except her first encounter with Soviet soldiers.
She had not forgotten; she simply could not relive the pain by
committing it to paper. Certainly she cannot be blamed for the
need to spare herself, but the chronicler of the history of
Winzig cannot be granted such leave. The events concerning
the entrance of Soviet troops into Winzig are an essential part
of that history. The record of the Russian troops as they
crossed into German lands constitutes a harsh indictment. But
the judgment of history must be tempered by understanding. It
is too facile to simply say that actions speak for themselves,
because that would give an incomplete picture. The results
must not be too far removed from their causes. The crimes
committed by Soviet military personnel must not be viewed out
of context. And the context consists of unspeakable atrocities
committed by the Germans in the Soviet Union. Upon crossing
into German soil, the rage of many Soviet soldiers was
unchained in an orgy of hatred. Everything German was
abhorrent. Every German was responsible for the war. Always
illogical, revenge is a powerful propellant toward ignoble
action. And there was much to avenge. The Soviet Union
suffered greater losses in the war than all other participants,
Allied and Axis, combined.

Not all Winzigers obeyed the order to evacuate. About
thirty refused to leave their homes. Most of them were old and
sick.   Fear of the unknown dangers of the open road was
greater than their fear of the Soviets. The circumstances
concerning Dr. Loele, his wife, and their young housekeeper,

however, were extraordinary. The doctor believed that his professional services would be useful to friend as well as foe and would grant him immunity from harm. Since his anti-Nazi politics were well known in the community, he persuaded himself that the Soviets would value his skill and his life. On the evening before the first Soviet soldiers stormed into town, the doctor discussed his rationale with Hugo Kliem, on old friend who had also decided to ignore the command to evacuate. During that last meeting between the two men, Dr. Loele referred to the poisons so neatly arranged in his medical supply cabinet. As a last resort, suicide, quick and painless, was his final option.

Hugo's tiny, wizened wife was too ill to travel, so the couple remained in their house on the Vorstadt. Kliem survived the first onslaught of enemy troops and provided a firsthand account of the confrontation between the remnant of Winzigers and a segment of Konev's army. A paraphrased synopsis of Hugo's narration follows:

There were no German soldiers around Winzig when a detachment of Konev's army entered on January 23. The nearest battle was around the Oder bridge in Steinau. Although the civilians huddling in their homes posed no threat to the invaders, the Soviet troops either did not realize this or did not care. Twelve of the residents were killed, probably on the first day of occupation. It was never known whether the shootings were ordered by officers or were carried out by soldiers who acted on their own. It is safe to assume that none of the old and sick Winzigers provoked the wrath of the invaders. It is reasonable, but by no means certain, that members of the Red Army killed the civilians in acts of individual violence. It was Kliem's clear impression that the shootings were done without fear of reprimand or court-martial; no inquiry was made to ascertain the facts surrounding the deaths. Something about Kliem, perhaps his white beard and defiant attitude, must have impressed the Soviet captain in charge. With the aid of his translator, he questioned Kliem concerning his political views. Apparently the captain was satisfied, because he settled down in Kliem's house and made it his temporary headquarters. Kliem and his wife were allotted one room for their use and were not molested by the soldiers. As thousands of Germans in occupied eastern Germany were to learn very soon, the protection of an officer was essential in the prevention of multiple rapes and in the preservation of life itself during the chaotic first days and weeks of occupation.

Kliem worried about the Loeles. He needed to see for himself how they fared during the first days of occupation. When he walked through the doctor's front door, his heart grew heavy in his chest. The always immaculate stairway was muddied from many boots. In the doctor's waiting room the furniture had been smashed. Then he saw three bodies sprawled in the surgery. Hugo Kliem wept as he straightened the widespread legs of the dead women. From the expression on the faces of his friends, he assumed that they had taken their own lives. The rapes had been committed upon corpses.[20]

Kliem feared that the bodies of the two women might still be used by Soviet soldiers, and the thought haunted him. He was old and very weak, but driven by the terrible images in his mind, he went back to the Loeles' house several nights after his first gruesome discovery. He took with him a spade and small handcart, the kind he had used to deliver milk to the creamery in another lifetime. One by one he dragged the stiffened bodies down the narrow staircase, heaved them onto the cart, and pulled his dismal load to the cemetery. The ground was frozen and Kliem was exhausted but he would not abandon his task until he had scratched a shallow grave for his three friends.[21]

The livestock left behind by the fleeing farmers was slaughtered by the Soviets. Even Kliem could not persuade his captain to spare his animals. Some of the cattle were used to feed the troops but much of the butchering was senseless. The intent was clear; destroy the means of future German survival. That meant that later waves of Soviet troops soon would find the larder empty.

Winzig as well as many other Silesian towns was not occupied by a permanent command. Rather they were used as brief way-stations for the masses of soldiers moving west. Each incoming group plundered the homes and barns until nothing was left. As new officers commanded the local scene, different rules and regulations applied to the civilians. Kliem and his wife were banned to a small, unheated attic room of their house, other Winzigers were driven entirely from their homes. Beatings were commonplace, and no woman, regardless of age or appearance, dared to show herself.

Close upon the heels of the regular army, Winzig was invaded by an army of a different sort. Kliem called them joy-girls and noted that among them many different nationalities were represented. He judged them severely, but we know nothing of the circumstances that caused these women to become camp followers and will refrain from any judgment. Apparently protected by the Soviet soldiers, they made themselves at home in Winzig's bedrooms and kitchens and remained as long as there were soldiers interested in their services.

On the 28 of January the fires began. Most of the houses around the Ring and the city hall burned to the ground. Fires also leveled much of the Vorstadt and the Bahnhofstrasse, as well as the hospital. Within a few weeks, ninety-four buildings were reduced to ashes. Kliem believed that the men of the Red Army committed deliberate arson. Other survivors blamed the careless disregard for safety with which the soldiers built fires to keep warm.[22] Perhaps both points of view contain some truth.

In the irrationality of war, the public utilities were destroyed. For years to come Winzig would be without electricity and without running water or gas. Neither the skilled manpower nor the necessary equipment would be available for decades in order to repair the damage.

Some of the people of Winzig who had heeded the evacuation order were unwilling to travel very far from town. They had no destinations in mind and hid wherever they could when the Red Army was near. For weeks or months they criss-crossed the familiar terrain, sleeping in barns and sometimes in the dense woods. The home and land they had abandoned exerted upon them a magnetic force, keeping them wandering within a well-defined orbit. Alois Stiller, a farmer from the Vorstadt, stayed within fifty kilometers of his house. Unfit for military duty because of an immense hernia that spilled over his trousers down to his knees, he left just ahead of the Soviets. After several weeks alone or among strangers, he decided in February to return. Did his house and barns still stand? Had any cattle survived? Of course, it was dangerous to be back on the road, but even his horse and wagon seemed propelled by his longing for home.

Alois was among the first of a streamlet of Winzigers who filtered back that winter and early spring. They expected to reestablish some form of their accustomed life of hard work and deprivations. But they would be on their own soil. Whatever the hopes of the returnees, they quickly turned into disillusionment. The Winzigers arrived in a state of shock from the hardships of the flight only to find that they owned absolutely nothing. All property left behind had been confiscated by the Soviet military authority. Furthermore, the returnees' very existence depended on the willingness of the occupation forces to let them live, to permit them to dig for the half-frozen potatoes they ate that winter and be housed in the sheds and huts assigned to them. Each new arrival was greeted with bittersweet joy, to be educated at once to the realities of life as a conquered people. Alois recounted that, despite the hunger, cold and the constant insecurity, the growing band of Winzigers shared their stories, food, and clothing with unforgettable comraderie.

The Germans who had lived through the Red Army invasion generally viewed the Soviets en masse as objects of hate and fear. It was simpler, more comfortable to apply the broadest stroke of the brush; "they" were uncivilized brutes. To admit that individual Soviet soldiers differed widely in character and behavior required the capacity to reject blind hatred and sweeping judgments. No doubt it was difficult for survivors of the first breakthrough of the Red Army to credit any of the invaders with humanitarian acts. But such acts of kindness were performed. Alois Stiller gave the following testimony:

> When the evacuation was ordered, Frau Sirp, an elderly woman, had been unable to leave home. When she heard shots being fired, she ran hysterically into the fields, where she collapsed. Russian soldiers found her nearly frozen to death. They turned her over to their medics who nursed her back to health.[23]

Soviet control of German territory east of the Oder-Neisse line was short-lived. In the ensuing months the region was gradually turned over to Polish authorities. In the case of

Winzig, Poles were given official control on May 22, 1945. Actually, both Soviets and Poles formed a joint administration until the late summer. Other Silesian towns experienced the substitution of command somewhat earlier as well as later in 1945.

Several generalizations concerning the months of Soviet occupation emerge from the abundance of eyewitness reports:

1. The first impact of the invading troops was the most dangerous moment for the population. Civilians were shot; property was destroyed without pattern, plan, or purpose. Although looting was common, only small items, such as watches, were carried away by the soldiers. Larger items soon had to be abandoned along the road during the westerly movements of the troops.

2. Women were raped without concern or consideration for age or appearance. Many victims felt that the Soviet troops treated such sexual abuse as a victor's justly earned prerogative. In Winzig, three women who sought refuge in the ruins of the house of the veterinarian, Dr. Schote, lived through months of sexual terror. Their experiences were repeated thousands of times from the border to Berlin.

3. In the occupied east the few remaining men, and in some areas even the strongest women, disappeared to do slave labor in the Soviet Union. Although the age limits for deportation differed somewhat from locality to locality, the effect was the same: only the weakest were left behind. The fate of the deported workers depended on where they were sent, what functions they performed and how their taskmasters chose to treat them. Many thousands never returned. Some were shipped as far away as Siberia. In the overcrowded trains, hunger, cold, typhoid and bloody diarrhea exacted death tolls as high as 50 percent. Those who endured were, for the most part, permitted to go home within a year or two.[24]

In Winzig, all men under the age of seventy were scraped together for slave labor. Even the misshapen Alois Stiller was slated to go. He was saved by an amazing coincidence. A man of Russian parentage who had lived in Winzig years ago returned to the town as a translator for the Soviets. He remembered Alois and struck his name from the deportation list.

4. A considerable number of evacuees returned to their eastern German hometowns and villages after the German surrender on May 8. These Silesians and East and West Prussians were unaware of the negotiations among the victorious powers that gave the Soviet Union a free hand in the eastern territories. For the most part, the Silesian returnees were those who had followed the southerly evacuation route to Czechoslovakia. When that area fell to the Soviet Union, they decided it was better to live in defeat at home than among the unfriendly Bohemians.[25]

5. The Soviet occupation administrators made no appreciable effort to distinguish between Nazi and anti-Nazi Germans. All were held equally responsible for the disaster of Hitler's regime. Clearly, those Germans who had suffered under the Nazi felt betrayed. When Polish occupation forces replaced the Soviets, this policy was continued.

6. The abuses suffered by the Silesian population cannot be attributed to military necessity. With the exception of the city of Breslau, the area fell without significant fighting. No resistance was offered by civilians, no snipers, no refusal to obey orders. If one word could describe the state of mind of the defeated eastern Germans that word would be fear.

In May of 1945 the semiofficial count of returned Winzigers was 81. A year later their number was 450. Often they came home to die. Both the Soviet and Polish administrators required hard work from the survivors in return for scant rations and inadequate shelter. The death toll from nutritional deprivation and lack of medical facilities was obviously high. The daily allotment for working adults was 300 grams of nonfat food plus 300 grams of dry bread. Children received nothing at all. Those over seventy were given provisions until July. After that, they received no more rations. When typhoid hit Winzig the mortality rate soared. Karl Schwerdtner, a man well respected for a lifetime of devotion to the Lutheran church, recorded events during these disastrous months. His diary shows this entry for September 6, 1945:

> We have deaths every day. . . . The dead are placed into plain coffins and rolled to the cemetery in two-wheeled carts. . . . Often without mourners; the old are too weary, the young must go to work.[26]

Among the victims to be placed in a grave in the Protestant cemetery was Hugo Kliem's twenty-four-year-old daughter-in-law. Her's was one of the daily funerals during the month of September. The contagion abated in October, and it was possible to conduct the internments with some dignity. By virtue of the single-minded Schwertdner and a sympathetic Polish commander, the devastated church was cleaned and the cows driven from the chapel in the cemetery.

The documentation of Winzigers confirmed that 1945 was their most calamitous year. Meeting the most essential, almost primitive needs for food, shelter, and medicine created overwhelming problems. Their bodies were underfed, overtired, and easy prey to illness. After the typhoid came scabies. As the months since the first breakthrough added up, unwanted babies were born to the rape victims. Especially among the young girls, the death rate due to childbirth complications was high. In addition, the returnees had to cope with crushing emotional problems. Where were the missing members of their families? That, of course, was the overriding concern. What would become of them? Every conversation between old neighbors questioned their own and their homeland's future. When would a peace treaty be written? How long would the occupation forces remain on German soil? Surely the pre-Nazi boundaries of Germany would be recognized.

But there were some disquieting signs. Polish families were moving onto some of the farms. They brought their tools and livestock, as if Winzig was going to be their permanent home. Many of these arrivals had been uprooted themselves. They had been forced to migrate from eastern Poland. Their land and homesteads were recently handed over to Soviet farmers. What did these population transfers mean?

By February of 1946, Polish sovereignty was complete and the Soviets withdrew from Winzig and adjoining districts. The Polish authorities demanded rent from the Winzigers living in parts of their own or someone else's house, to be collected retroactively to July 1945. But even the most insistent tax collector cannot exact money from people who have nothing. It was not an auspicious beginning.

Despite the political, economic, and emotional obstacles, civil life was reawakened in Winzig during the Polish interval. It centered about the church. Father Willinek had not been permitted to return from his Bavarian refuge, but the Protestant minister had made his way back. Reverend Boerner was in his seventies and in poor health, but his resolve was strong. With the aid of Karl Schwerdtner, he restored the church and its weekly services. Since he was the only minister in the entire county, he met the needs of a widespread flock. His work was crowned in March of 1946, when the church rang with the prayer and song of a large congregation celebrating the confirmation of forty children.

Spring gave the optimists a ray of renewed hope. Many of the 450 Germans in Winzig were permitted to return to their empty homes and overgrown gardens. Hoes, rakes, and precious seed were shared, as vegetable gardens were restored. Some of the farmers plowed and sowed their land-a remarkable effort with scant equipment and few workers. Though there was still no mail, nor electric or gas power, no doctor or pharmacist, no school, no Catholic church or goods in the shops, the land was there with its promise of a harvest.

There was even cause to commend the Polish authorities in their handling of the timberlands. The vicinity of Winzig had beautiful and valuable forests, and the Polish District Control reinstated the former chief forester, Guenzel, to his position. He was permitted to return to his fairy tale house in the woods and encouraged to preserve and plant in the best tradition of his profession. The eighty men of his work force were not unhappy slave laborers but were paid a decent wage. Perhaps an omen for a better future?

The answer to that question came soon enough. The farmers had often wondered who would eat the fruits of their labor. Now they knew. As soon as most of the meager harvest was in, the sword of Damocles fell upon the Silesians, the East and West Prussians, and the Pomeranians living east of the Oder-Neisse Line. The uncertainty, the endless and conflicting rumors, were finally laid to rest. The Polish government had decided to expel the approximately 3 million returnees. From East Prussia to Upper Silesia, notices were posted: Germans must leave within a few hours or, at best, a few days. Assembly points were designated, weight restrictions for portable personal property issued, and transportation was provided. But before boarding the trains or trucks, the ex-patriates were subjected to several so-called "searches for weapons" of their bundles. Actually, the Polish militia used this opportunity to steal whatever items took their fancy.[27] As will be discussed in the following chapter, arrangements had been made with the British occupation administration to receive the dispossessed into their zone of western Germany.

The day of departure for the people of Winzig was August 16, 1946. With so few possessions, packing required little effort. Leaving the land of one's ancestors was quite another matter. The farmers walked their familiar fields one more time. If they were left with nothing else, these memories must be sharp and clear. The Polish newcomers, so recently ejected from their own land, understood. Several tried to express their sympathy. Then a pathetic line formed to wind its way to the railroad station. When the last of the group boarded the train, the little German town of Winzig died. In its place new maps indicate a Polish village. Its name is Winsco.

6

The Oder-Neisse Line: Focus of Conflicting Claims

The people of Winzig who had been expelled by order of the Polish government in 1946 numbered about 450. They were but a small fraction of a total of approximately 3,500,000 eastern Germans who were forced to leave their homeland at this juncture. Some 6 million had moved westward earlier to escape the Soviet armies and had not returned after the armistice. The fate of the little group bidding tearful farewells to the familiar sights of Winzig was but a single word among the countless pages attesting to the enormous cost of German aggression. What price, what value can be assessed the 35 million lives lost in the war? How could the destruction of property on three continents be estimated? When the truth of the Holocaust with its death factories became agonizingly clear, the world reacted with revulsion. Even now, almost a half century later, the planned mass murder of 11 million innocent civilians defies the sane mind and strains the human imagination.

It is very difficult to be rational about the atrocious crimes of the Hitler era. An entire generation of Nazis and their collaborators have to die out to blur the stain. The convictions won by the Nuremberg and other war crimes tribunals served as tokens of retribution, useful, perhaps, only as symbols. World War II brought anguish to hundreds of millions, and among them were Germans. Their country was in ruins, their families suffered great losses, and the shame of their crimes lay open to the world. Whether guilty or innocent of supporting the Nazi terror, blame fell on all Germans indiscriminately.

Hatred for the German people created an attitude of indifference, even glee toward their suffering. This lack of sympathy
was extended to old and young, the hungry and the ill. The
eastern population expelled from their homes was not viewed
by the Allies as deserving any consideration in this post-war
atmosphere. The acquiescence by the victorious powers in
dismembering eastern Germany must be viewed within the
context of the devastation the Nazis had inflicted on the
Western world. The expulsion was unjust, particularly since no
effort was made to ascertain the political views and activities
of those ordered to leave their homes. Nazis and anti-Nazis
alike, the Spielers and the Langs, lost their property and their
homeland. They were equally guilty. They were Germans.

The dispossessed population knew little and cared less
about the international politics that resulted in their homeless-
ness. It sufficed to understand that they were victims of a lost
war. A new boundary had been drawn, and they were helpless
to resist the expulsion. While great men made great decisions,
their concerns dealt with the consequences and how to survive
them.

The current map of Europe resulted from wartime conferences among the Allied leaders. The Big Three, at their
meetings in Tehran, Yalta, and Potsdam, were confronted with
military problems vital to winning the war as well as with
postwar issues. Stalin, Churchill, Roosevelt, and later Truman
had to respond to a multitude of domestic, strategic, and
foreign policy problems. The decisions that permitted the
western expansion of Poland were made during a devastating
war, a war unquestionably unleashed by Hitler. Indeed, the
Nazis were culpable, but surely the soldiers were German
soldiers. They fired weapons made in German factories, and the
political views of those who made the guns or those who fired
them were immaterial. "Nazi" and "German" were joined
concepts that could not possibly be uncoupled until sometime
in the future. For the moment, hatred for all who had lived
under the swastika was elevated to righteousness and patriotism.
Later, with the wisdom of hindsight, criticism was voiced
concerning some of the decisions made by the Allied leadership. The fairness or unfairness of such censure is not at issue
here, but it is appropriate to recall the prevailing climate of the

war years.

Poland today stretches from the north-south flow of the Bug River in the east to the Oder-Neisse Line in the west. Neither the Curzon Line on her frontier with the Soviet Union nor Poland's border with East Germany was determined by specific agreements among the Allies. The boundaries evolved because they suited Stalin and his vision of postwar eastern Europe. The Soviet leader decided to shear off Eastern Poland at the Bug along a line first suggested by the British foreign secretary, Lord Curzon, in 1919. German lands east of the Oder and Neisse rivers would then be proffered to offset Polish losses.

Certain historical claims have been offered to justify this shift in the Silesian frontier. The assertion that Poland had ancient legitimate rights to the so-called recovered region was no more or no less justifiable than other challenges that could be made for many border areas in central Europe. At the height of the Piast dynasty, during the tenth and eleventh centuries, the region was Polish. It passed into the hands of the Bohemian crown, and when that was lost to the Austrian Hapsburgs so was Silesia. In the eighteenth century the Prussian king, Frederick the Great, wrested Silesia from Austria. Thus for six hundred years Silesia had not been a Polish possession.[1] At the end of World War I, Germany lost the province of Posen and parts of Upper Silesia to Poland at the peace settlement of Versailles. These areas had a sizable Polish minority. The population of greater Silesia, however, which remained in the Reich, was German. The language, the customs, the nationalism were German. Polish assertions to the contrary do not change these facts.

The current German-Polish boundary was derived from two fundamental sources. First was the military victory by the Soviet Union and her subsequent relinquishment of the land to the Poles. This was discussed in the previous chapter. Poland, with the complete support of the Soviet Union, was in possession of the land, and only an unthinkable military action could dislodge her. This factor was enough to override any debate on the subject among the Allies. The second element in creating the current status consisted of the conferences of the Big Three. Their decisions-or lack thereof-had essential bearing upon the revisions of the map of Poland.

As far back as the Tehran Conference in 1943, Stalin insisted that the Curzon Line along the Bug River should become Soviet Union's western border as part of the eventual postwar settlement. That line had been favored by the Allies in 1919 when modern Poland was reestablished. Lenin, facing grave territorial losses all along the western frontier, had refused to accept Lord Curzon's proposal. A brief armed clash between Polish and Soviet forces then ensued in 1920, and a settlement was reached at the Treaty of Riga. The Ukrainian and Byelorussian territories were divided, giving Poland more than Lord Curzon had suggested but less than the Polish government had hoped for.[2] For the time being the Soviet Union had to accept the loss of a traditionally Russian area, but the desire to make some future readjustment never diminished.

The next reshaping of Poland's eastern boundaries took place in 1939, just after the German victory over that hapless land. In accordance with the Hitler-Stalin nonaggression pact, signed during the summer of that year, the Soviet Union annexed the territory between her existing frontier and the Curzon Line. At that moment, when Hitler was teaching the world the meaning of *Blitzkrieg*, neither Poland nor her allies, that is, France and England, were in any position to effectively protest this seizure.

The German attack on the Soviet Union in 1941 resulted in the rapid conquest of much of European Russia, including the area recently seized from Poland. During the next four years, the U.S.S.R. and her people suffered unprecedented losses. At the Tehran Conference of 1943, Stalin's most pressing demand of Churchill and Roosevelt was for military relief. He pleaded for the immediate opening of a second front, an Allied invasion in the west, which would ease the pressure of German armies in the east. But the Soviet leader did not fail to touch upon the perpetually critical question of his country's western boundaries. He requested that U.S.S.R.'s postwar boundaries run along the Curzon Line. Churchill and Roosevelt agreed to this proposal but it was designated as a preliminary decision. The first momentous agreement, though secret and tentative, had been reached which would eventually lead to enormous population shifts.

Early in 1945 the Big Three met at Yalta. At that point, Germany's defeat was close at hand. The realization that his nation had borne the major brunt of Nazi aggression gave Stalin considerable advantage in the deliberations. The war was not yet won, and numerous military and strategic problems called for resolutions. But beyond that, the awesome task of outlining the shape of Europe's future rested upon the Allied leaders. The creation of a peacekeeping organization, so auspiciously and so deceptively, called the United Nations, was well under way. The proposed division of Germany into zones of occupation was on the table, requiring agreement. A further challenge for the heads of state was Poland and how the long-suffering Polish people could attain justice, security, and economic viability. If it were possible to speak of the rape of a nation, Poland had been raped by the Germans. Six million of her citizens had been killed, her economy destroyed, and her surviving population reduced to slave labor. The Polish bound-ary discussions were colored by these realities. Stalin insisted that the Soviet Union retain its land acquisition of 1939. This westerly advance of the Soviet border was to be incorporated into the eventual peace settlement. Polish losses would be compensated at Germany's expense. Thus the Oder-Neisse Line was born. Vyacheslav Molotov, Stalin's Foreign Minister, made this statement after consultation with the Polish leadership during the Yalta Conference:

1. It was agreed that the Curzon Line should be the eastern frontier of Poland, with adjustments in some regions of five to eight kilometers in favor of Poland.
2. It was decided that the western frontier should be drawn from the town of Stettin (which would be Polish) and thence outhward along the Oder and western Neisse rivers.[3]

The memoirs of Prime Minister Churchill recount the discussion at Yalta concerning the millions (at that time the number was believed to be 6 instead of 10 million) of eastern Germans who would have to be moved. Churchill thought it might be managed, subject to the moral question, which he

would have to settle with his own people. Stalin's reply was
rather prophetic. He said that there are no Germans in that
territory inasmuch as they had all run away.[4]

Churchill expressed his doubt that Germany could absorb
such a stream of refugees. But Stalin countered that such
absorption was entirely feasible. He claimed that the Germans
had already lost 6 or 7 million of their population and another
2 million were likely to be killed before the war ended. In
view of these losses, the refugees could certainly be accommodated in the remaining German lands.[5] Clearly Stalin had
won the day. The official communique on the conference was
issued on February 13, 1945. Section VII dealt with the
question at hand and read as follows:

> The three heads of Government consider that the
> eastern frontier of Poland should follow the Curzon line
> with digressions in some regions of five to eight
> kilometers in favor of Poland.
>
> They recognize that Poland must receive a substan-
> tial compensation of territory in the north and west.
> They feel that the opinion of the Polish Provisional
> Government of National Unity should be sought out in
> due course of the extent of these awards and that the
> final delineation of the western frontier of Poland
> should therefore await the peace conference.[6]

References to the prospective peace conference occurred
frequently in the deliberations of the Allies. It seemed reasonable that problems that could not be settled in the atmosphere of
wartime emergencies would be dealt with at a later, more quiet
time. But the spirit of Allied cooperation, so vital to the defeat
of the Axis powers, soon faded and blurred and then evapora-
ted altogether. Consequently, no peace conference was ever
called to settle the future of Germany. The notion of drafting
a World War II settlement now, nearly a half century after the
armistice, suggests a page from *Alice in Wonderland*.

In July of 1945, about two months after the end of
hostilities, the Allied heads of state met again. Franklin D.
Roosevelt had died, and Pres. Harry S. Truman, a relative
newcomer to international politics, represented the United

States. Two days after the meeting convened at Potsdam, Winston Churchill received the news that the British voters had turned him out and the new PM, Clement Attlee, would replace him as the English spokesman.

Of the Big Three who had met at Yalta, only Stalin remained. Germany was the paramount topic at the conference. It was now necessary to affix administrative particulars to the rather general accord of the Crimean meeting. The military occupation of Germany and its division into four zones was viewed as a stopgap measure to bridge Hitler's Third Reich to the vision of a future Germany that would be free, democratic, and unified. During the occupation interregnum, much had to be accomplished. Fascists, militarists, and economic cartels had to be eradicated. At the same time, encouragement was to be offered to the democratic, peaceloving segment of the German population, who would be vital to the regeneration of the country. When, in the judgment of the Allies, the German people were ready to take their place among the sovereign nations of the world, a peace conference would then be called to settle all outstanding problems.[7]

The Potsdam meeting was an attempt to paper over the rifts that had begun to undermine Allied unity. With Soviet troops at the Elbe, the bargaining power of the Soviet Union had further increased. The Western Allies, on the other hand, were sensitive to their people's exhaustion and their desperate desire for peace. The United States, strongest among the powers, did not know how long her costly struggle with Japan might yet continue. Stalin was well aware of his position when he presented the conference with a fait accompli: his cession of the Oder-Neisse territory to Poland.[8] Clearly, this unilateral action went beyond the language and the spirit of Allied understanding.

The United States knew of the Soviet Union's cession before the Potsdam convention met. As early as April 1945 it protested to the Soviet government, but it received a rather curt reply from the vice commissar of foreign affairs: "The administration of these territories was presupposed at Yalta and thus there has been no breach of agreement.[9]

The Western Allies, hoping to preserve a semblance of concord, did not take a firm stand on the issue. Stalin thus achieved an easy victory. How far would the Soviet leader have gone to assure Poland of its prize if his wartime allies had objected more vigorously? An interesting but fruitless speculation.

Although the Potsdam Agreement provided guidelines for the removal of German civilians from Poland, Czechoslovakia, and Hungary, no mention was made of the expulsion of Germans from their own land. On the matter of reparations, paragraphs I and II stipulated that:

> I. Reparation claims shall be met by removals from the zone of Germany occupied by the U.S.S.R. and from appropriate German external assets.
> II. The U.S.S.R. undertakes to settle the reparations claims of Poland from its own share of reparation.[10]

No figure was set for the amount or the value of goods designated as reparations, nor were provisions made for international supervision of the method of collection. A point completely ignored by the conferring parties was the fact that east of the Oder-Neisse rivers, Soviet and Polish forces had already carried off everything valuable. An inventory of items confiscated included livestock, particularly horses, machinery, and all types of vehicles. Factories, even houses were dismantled to supply bricks for the rebuilding of devastated areas in the U.S.S.R. In addition, goods disappeared from shops, utensils from kitchens, and clothing from closets. It is doubtful that anyone could estimate which items became reparation payments and which disappeared into the pockets of Soviet and Polish looters.

No point of the deliberations at Potsdam was more important to the dispersed Silesians than the boundary question. No point produced greater frustration. Section IX B of the agreement is excerpted below:

> The following agreement was reached on the western frontier of Poland:
> In conformity with the agreement on Poland reached at the Crimean Conference the three heads of government have sought the opinions of the Polish Provisional Government of National Unity at the Conference in

regard to the accession of territory in the north and west which Poland should receive. The President of the National Council of Poland and the Members of the Polish Provisional Government of National Unity at the conference have fully expressed their views. The three heads of government reaffirm their opinions that the final delineation of the western frontier of Poland should await the peace settlement. The three heads of state agree that, pending the final determination of Poland's western frontier, the former German territories east of the line running from the Baltic Sea just west of Swinemunde, and thence along the Oder River to the confluence of the western Neisse to the Czechoslovak frontier, including that portion of East Prussia not placed under the administration of the Union of Soviet Socialist Republics in accordance with the understanding reached at this conference and including the area of the former free city of Danzig, shall be under the administration of the Polish State and for such purposes should not be considered part of the Soviet zone of occupation of Germany.[11]

Thus the de facto Polish border was confirmed on August 2, 1945. Would a peace conference have upheld the line? Probably, and for two reasons. First, the Polish government settled her own citizens into the "reclaimed" area and any alteration of the frontier would entail another distressing dislocation of people. Second, history instructs us that, unless dispossessed by force, victors usually retain their spoils.

More recent developments have supported this presumption. East Germany assented to the eastern boundary in a treaty with Poland signed on July 6, 1950. It is symbolic that the agreement was signed in a city now divided by the Oder-Neisse Line, called Goerlitz on one side, Zgorzelec on the other. West Germany, under Chancellor Willy Brandt and his Social Democratic party, acceded to the existing line in an accord that, in part, stated:

The Polish People's Republic and the Federal Republic of Germany unanimously affirm that the existing border

line, the course of which was established in Chapter IX
of the decisions of the Potsdam Conference.[12]

Predictably, the organizations formed in West Germany by
the men and women dispossessed from the eastern territories
protested vehemently. They saw this treaty as a sellout of their
ancient homeland, but despite their objections, the Bundestag
confirmed it.

The eastern losses were further upheld in 1970, when the
West German and Polish governments concluded a pact known
as the Warsaw Treaty. The agreement established the Oder-
Neisse as Poland's western boundary "in letter and in spirit."
The two countries promised to lodge no territorial claims
against each other and vowed the "inviolability of their existing
borders, now and in the future."[13]

As we enter the last decade of this century, we witness
incredible changes. The newly achieved political unity of West
and East Germany generated nervous concern in the Polish
government. Will a united, democratic Germany seek to reopen
negotiations concerning its eastern boundary? Will the increased
size, population, and power of a single Germany be followed
by demands for the reestablishment of the 1937 borders?
Would German political parties hope to appeal to voters by
promoting changes in the frontier?

The disintegration of Soviet unity, and the decline of
communist power throughout the world has left the former
satellite nations unprotected. If the current German Government
decided to use force to regain its prewar boundaries, only the
moral power of the United Nations and, perhaps, the military
power of the U.S. could prevent such a move.

Is such a maneuver likely? The answer, at this time, is a
resounding NO! Despite the ultra-right wing German Republican party, (a splinter group whose platform includes the
restoration of pre-Nazi borders), the political leaders representing the majority views are committed to retaining the status
quo. This position was borne out again when Helmuth Kohl,
chancellor of the Federal Republic, and Polish prime minister
Tadeusze Mazowiecki signed a joint declaration on November
14, 1989, that renewed Bonn's guarantee to fulfill the pledge

given in the Warsaw Treaty.[14]

The Polish government had gone to extraordinary lengths to legitimize the annexation in its western region. Although in square mileage Poland lost more to the Soviet Union than she gained from Germany, the acquired land was far more valuable. From every point of view, industrially, agriculturally, and strategically, the western area surpassed her eviction along the river Bug. The Oder-Neisse region, that is, the western part of East Prussia, East Pomerania, East Brandenburg, and Silesia, has become vital to Poland's economy and this may well explain her desire to establish unimpeachable title to it. The agency which administered the area until 1950, (when the differences between the new and old lands were abolished), was named the Ministry of Recovered Territories.[15] The Polish Tourist Bureau extolled the beauty and charm of the ancient Polish city of Wroclaw, formerly and better known as the Silesian capital of Breslau. Historic accounts stressed the medieval sovereignty of Polish kings and asserted that traditionally Silesia's poor were Polish and the oppressive rich were German. The sample below makes the case in point:

> The struggle in defense of Polish nationalism in Silesia was distinctly in the nature of a national liberation struggle, as in that territory peasants, workers and the low middle class were Polish while the well-to-do and the governing classes were German. In light of the most recent investigations, industrial and agricultural workers constitute 90% of the Polish population of Silesia.[16]

Such pretensions are suitable for the realm of a publicist, not a historian. There are simply too many people who lived in Silesia and know better. Other attempts to justify the westerly advance of the Polish border were equally thin. For example, in a treatise called "The Polish-German Frontier, Law Life and Logic of History," published in Warsaw in 1964, Manfred Lachs alleged that Poland's claim to the Oder-Neisse Line was valid because the Potsdam Agreement granted her the right of "administration," which is but another term for "sovereignty":

Administration, therefore, as opposed to "Occupation"
implied the permanent character of the authority, thus
becoming equivalent to the word "Sovereignty". And it
cannot be denied that it has been frequently used in the
past to convey this meaning.[17]

The preoccupation of Polish writers in defending the
possession of the western frontier found frequent exposition in
the publication *Polish Western Affairs*. Every historic, legal, and
humanitarian claim was used to assert the validity of the
acquisition. One often repeated presumption claimed that
"Cessation of Hostilities" can be interpreted as "peace settlement." Such verbal acrobatics were then applied to reshape the
assessment of the Potsdam Agreement; it became a "peace
treaty."[18] The inane assertion that Germany ceded the territory
of her own free will is not worthy of discussion and merely
points up the excesses of such attempts at official rationali-
zation.

In this last decade of the century, the question of the
eastern territories is no longer a matter of serious international
significance. The land is Polish because it is the home of
Polish people. Culture develops from the human environment,
not from geographical contours or lines drawn across the map
by politicians far removed from the scene. Soil has no nationa-
lity: only people do. It no longer matters that Hugo Kliem was
deeply attached to the farm worked by his family for hundreds
of years. His children and their children now live in West
Germany. In his house in Winsco, a Polish mother, perhaps
born in Winsco, sings a Polish lullaby to her baby. Ten million
Poles through their lives and labors have made this area a part
of Poland; such is the decree of realism and humanitarianism.

The resettlement of the millions of displaced people from
the eastern lands constituted a remarkable chapter of recent
history. Germany was a ruined country, defeated and shamed,
yet its people found the heart and habitation to accommodate
the refugees. The occupation authorities extended help, but the
resettlement of such large numbers of impoverished, bewildered
newcomers was largely a German success. The western zones,
later the Federal Republic, received and accepted the bulk of
the fleeing population. As long as there was a choice among

the French, English, American, or Russian zones, the over-whelming majority opted for the West. The influx ended only when the Soviet government insisted on a ban against further flight from her zone.

As was noted previously, the first evacuation of the area east of the Oder-Neisse was ordered by the German authorities to escape the Soviet armies. Only a portion of the escaping population returned after the armistice. In Winzig, with a prewar population of 2,000, roughly 500, or one-fourth, made their way back and remained until the final expulsion in 1946. These figures were representative of the ratio for all the detached territories. The eastern provinces held 10 million inhabitants during the war. One can only guess how many residents refused the order to leave or were overrun by enemy troops before they could flee. At the time the area was granted to Poland, approximately 3,500,000 Germans remained there. The earliest expulsions, those ordered in 1945, involved hundreds of thousands who were sent to the Russian Zone of Occupation. Most of these Germans were prevented by the Soviet government from moving farther west. Rektor Spieler, Winzig's courageous school principal, was among the thousands trying to get into the American Occupation Zone. With his worldly goods in a baby carriage, he and Frau Spieler walked through the Czech mountains to the Bavarian border. But the door had been slammed shut; he was not permitted to cross. He and his wife wearily trekked back to spend the rest of their lives in poverty under Communist rule.

One million Germans remained in the provinces acquired by Poland.[19] The protection of the rights of these ethnic Germans was an issue of the 1989 Joint Declaration concluded by the Polish and West German governments: "Warsaw . . . promised to allow the formation of associations enabling ethnic Germans there to cultivate their language, create their own libraries and media and receive support from the [German] Federal Republic."[20]

The intent of the Polish government to expatriate the German population in 1946 spurred the Allied Control Council into action. The council, representing the administration of all four zones of occupation, sought to make the evacuation as orderly and humane as possible. There had been a constant trickle of westward-fleeing Germans, but 1,375,000 had remained and now were to be driven out. When the British government declared its readiness to accept the refugees into its zone, a Polish-British commission was created to make the appropriate arrangements. Operation Swallow, known as Operation Schwalbe, was organized and successfully coordinated the transfer with a minimum of hardship for the evacuees.[21]

The people of Winzig were ordered to assemble in the nearby town of Goerlitz. In compliance with instructions they took only such baggage as they could carry in their hands. Few, if any, members of the group had the sum of 5,000 Reichsmarks (value about $200), which was the total amount the exiles were permitted to take with them. Friends and old neighbors boarded the trains together and disembarked at the same destination in Westphalia within the British Zone. With other arrivals from Lower Silesia, their journey ended in the Sauerland, a vacation area of great natural beauty. The town of Meschede was a focal point of the region and as former Winzigers settled down, it became their bridge between the old and the new life.

Former Winzigers, quite naturally, tried to stay near each other in their new surroundings. Who else could share their recollections of better times in the past? Or bring back their dead, even for a moment, by sharing a loving memory? Here, in Westphalia, they were outsiders. They were the people who spoke with an odd dialect, prepared meals in their own particular style, and referred to Silesia as if it had been the Garden of Eden. They were the newcomers who competed with the native-born population for jobs, housing, and public services. Winzigers and their counterparts from the eastern provinces experienced a wide range of reactions from the native Westphalians. Most often they were met with kindness; sometimes they experienced aloofness and indifference. Occasionally they were hurt by spitefulness and meanness. Although everyone had suffered, everyone had lost someone during the war, the essential nature of men and women remained unaltered in its variety.

After the end of the war, many German families searched for missing members of their households. Great confusion had been caused by the bombing of cities and the movement of children to so-called safe areas. In addition, discharged soldiers and armament workers were looking for their homes and relatives on rubbled streets they could no longer recognize. The difficulties in finding missing members of one's family multiplied for the displaced population from the Oder-Neisse Line. How could returning servicemen find them? Or released prisoners of war? Or discharged members of the Volkssturm? Or the slave laborers who had been sent to work in the Soviet Union and in Poland? Homeless wanderers, they would make their way to places like Winzig and find a handful of Polish farmers there. Agencies, such as the Red Cross, tried to deal with the massive movement of peoples across central Europe but could not cope with the millions seeking their help. Resourceful individuals left messages on lamp posts and under stones in the rubble where houses once stood: "Hans Mueller, come to Springerstrasse 17, Mutter and Ilse"; or "Anyone from Schmograu, Silesia, please, contact Hans Schmidt now at Kastanienallee 67."

The renewal of life was bound up in the renewal of family. Even the news of death was preferable to the searing uncertainty and endless waiting and hoping.

Father Willinek, Winzig's former Catholic priest, had been evacuated during the winter of early 1945. He tried to join the returnees in 1946 but was unable to arrange his reentry. Although of retirement age, he accepted an appointment to a parish not far from the Sauerland. In the course of his ministry, he came into contact with several of his Silesian neighbors. He saw in these chance meetings an opportunity to once again serve Winzigers, regardless of their religious affiliation, by helping to bring families and old friends together.

His work began with the gathering of names and addresses. His lists grew as his contacts widened. Sadly, the number of dead expanded alongside the roll call of the living. A printer, fortunate enough to have saved some of his machinery, joined the project in exchange for some groceries. The first mailing was distributed in March of 1946 and consisted of 150 names on a single sheet of paper. When Father Willinek added a commentary, he had, in fact, created a newsletter. He called it *Heimatklaenge* (Sounds of Home), and he described its purpose in these words:

One year ago we suffered the loss of our homeland,
and we greatly desire to establish contact with one
another by letter. This mailing is our first step intended
in that direction. It ought to reach all Winzigers and
those from the environs whose addresses are known to
me at this time. It is not my intention to place myself
in a special role in this undertaking. We are living in
an age of democracy. There are no leaders with self-
appointed rights. But someone must make a start, and
since no one else has begun this correspondence so far,
I set myself to the task, which I will turn over to
someone else if this be deemed desirable.[22]

For the rest of his life, the leadership of Winzigers in exile
remained largely in the hands of Father Willinek. When poor
health forced him to give up his pastoral duties, he continued
to devote his energies to the *Heimatklaenge*. His religious faith
was firmly linked to the belief that service to man was his first
duty. His physical heart weakened, but not his spirit. The single
sheet of names developed in size and format until it became a
small magazine, published several times a year. A handsome
masthead displayed a silhouette of prewar Winzig, and special
features began to appear. Personal news continued to play an
important role, and reminiscences of the lost life gave readers
a great deal of bittersweet pleasure. Poetry and prose, some
fairly dripping with homesickness, appeared quite regularly. But
the *Heimatklaenge's* entry into politics gave it a purpose and
a dimension beyond catering to the longing for the old *Heimat*.
The deportees from the Oder-Neisse Line wanted more than an
arena to vent their emotions, more than the preservation of their
rich cultural heritage. They wanted the return of their homeland. Only the restoration of the 1937 borders of Germany
could satisfy their hopes. Clearly, the means to accomplish this
end had to be political. Sentimental yearning for the past
needed to be converted into electoral clout. Votes, many
thousands of votes, might reach the ears of elected officials. To
exert such influence required organization that could blend
individual voices into a formidable chorus. In western Germany,
several political alliances, such as the Union of Silesians, and
the League of Expellees, actively championed the cause of the

ousted population. In the Communist east, of course, such agitation was forbidden.

Former Silesians, East and West Prussians, and Pomeranians had been scattered throughout the four occupation zones. In no geographic area did they comprise a majority of the population. In 1949 the three Western zones were combined as a preliminary step to the establishment of a sovereign nation, the West German Federal Republic. In the same year, the Soviet Union created the Communist satellite of East Germany, the German Democratic Republic. Contact between the people of the two Germanies grew difficult, and naturally joint political action became impossible. It was inconceivable that the Communist regime would permit political, or even social, agitation for the lands now held by her sister satellite, Poland.

In the west, however a unique cultural/political entity developed, the *Patenstadt*. Literally translated, the word means "godparent city." This concept of a home away from home was based on the willingness of a West German municipality to "adopt" a city or town lost to Poland. In practical terms, a number of privileges were granted to the expelled eastern Germans. For example, representatives were permitted to officially participate in civic functions. Records, art treasures, memorabilia, photos, and so forth, that had been rescued were granted accommodations for display and safe keeping, usually in the city hall. The godparent city also donated public sites for the erection of commemorative monuments to honor the history and the war dead of lost towns. Streets were named in memory of Silesian, Pomeranian, or eastern Prussian communities. Usually such dedication occasions were marked by solemn ceremonies. The *Patenstadt* became the center for the political and social activities of the displaced people who lived in and around the area. Here they often held their reunions, published their newspapers and focused their efforts to maintain their culture and strengthen their identity. Initially only the big cities sought sponsors. Breslau, for example, was accepted by Cologne. Larger towns followed suit. Wohlau, formerly a county seat, established its *Patenstadt* in Hilden. Many smaller villages and towns within a county joined together under the aegis of a single West German town. Before long the search for *Patenstaedte* reached down to the expatriates from the smallest communities. That, of course, included Winzigers. Largely due to the leadership of Father Willinek, they appealed to the citizens and town council of beautiful Meschede. Located west of Cologne in the Sauerland of Westphalia, Meschede was founded over a thousand years ago. Its history reflects the European past from the conversion to Christianity by missionaries sent by Charlemagne, to its destruction during the Thirty Years War, to its partial ruin during World War II. An ancient monastery and castle still stand, and the surrounding hills and forests have attracted nature lovers for centuries. Winzigers had staged five of their yearly reunions in Meschede before they requested the *Patenstadt* status. During this time the townspeople and administrators had come to know the Winzigers, their organization and their aims. They liked what they saw and accepted the charge to become Winzig's Patenstadt. Ten years after the expulsion, on June 10, 1956, Meschede's mayor, Engelbert Dick, proclaimed the agreement. He called on his fellow citizens to help their brothers and sisters who had lost their homeland to establish new homes in the area. In a speech to Winzigers he formally and solemnly declared that:

> with this undertaking the City Council of Meschede expresses its understanding of the fate of the East Germans and takes to its heart the welfare of the expellees and of the Germans in the Soviet zone. By accepting the guardianship it wishes to do its share in preparing for the day when Germany must be reunited.[23]

Father Willinek responded with expressions of gratitude and delineated for the five hundred attending Winzigers what the *Patenstadt* arrangement entailed. The services Meschede promised to perform included the following

1. The development and maintenance of personal, historical, and cultural memorabilia.
2. A room in the town hall available for Winzig's archives, flags, a model street plan, and such.
3. The mailing of the newsletter *Heimatklaenge*.

4. Provision of a suitable location for a memorial stone dedicated to Winzig's fallen soldiers.
5. Renaming a street Winzigerstrasse.
6. Providing aid for former Winzigers who are aged and sick.
7. Inclusion of young members of the exiled community in civic functions whenever feasible.[24]

All of these promises were kept. Less obvious, but perhaps more important, was the emotional and political support the *Patenstadt* accorded its wards. The official welcome and expressions of compassion were bound to secure stronger ties between Winzigers and native-born Sauerlanders. The people of Meschede, at best, might have had a passing interest in the eastern provinces, but the publicity related to the *Patenstadt* duties heightened their awareness. The expelled population needed and sought general public support for its political agenda. An endorsement of their aims, even one as cautiously phrased as Mayor Dick's, kept the issue of their homeland before the voters. And political persuasion was the chosen instrument of the banished eastern Prussians.

The generation that had suffered the actual expulsion resolved to work for the return of the Oder-Neisse lands. Their demands, however, were never couched in the violent language coming from the dispossessed of the Middle East. Never did the German refugees support the use of arms. Their title to the territory was more reasonable than most such historic claims; nonetheless, they shrank from the use of illegal tactics. Terrorism was viewed as an abhorrent form of political action, perhaps due to the lessons of the recent violent German history. In addition, there existed a strong ethical/religious element. Clean hands and a clear conscience were prerequisites to an eventual return. The old homeland could be rebuilt only by deserving, blameless, law-abiding Germans.

At the 1956 reunion of Winzigers, Father Willinek voiced the credo of his countrymen in these five points:

1. Our love for our homeland requires no words.
2. We do not want a war to satisfy our claims.
3. We plead with God and all people of goodwill to

make our return to the land of our fathers possible.
4. We will do everything possible in our new homes
   to be worthy of our return.
5. We will only return to Silesia untainted by Bolshevism.[25]

The tone of Father Willinek's words appealed to human
and religious principles, while the All-Silesian Assembly sought
legal grounds for the same claims when its membership
resolved that:

1. in accordance with international law, the expulsion
   of the Germans from their ancient homes within the
   German state was a breach of said law;
2. a crime has never created legal rights for the perpetrators but results in demands of the injured for
   restitution;
3. according to existing laws of nations, annexations
   are forbidden and conquest does not create ownership rights;
4. in accordance with international law no territorial
   changes can be undertaken without the consent of
   the affected population;
5. Soviet peace proposals try to establish that we,
   among all the peoples of the earth, be the only ones
   to be denied on a permanent basis the right to self-
   determination . . . ;
6. according to said design, the eastern provinces are
   to be denied their homelands and self-determin-
   ation.[26]

The above excerpt was written in 1959, when the wounds
of the expelled peoples were still fresh and the assimilation to
their new homes still tenuous. No doubt their call for justice
was legally sound and emotionally seductive. No doubt other
groups could make similar claims. No doubt if their demands
had been met, a series of valid counter claims would have been
created. A chain reaction, reaching to the western frontiers of
the Soviet Union, would have been unlocked, creating ever
greater problems and much human misery in its wake.

The bromide about time and its ability to heal was true for the Oder-Neisse population. Indeed, the world is either indifferent or oblivious to the events surrounding the establishment of the postwar boundary between Germany and Poland. It simply is not a headline-making issue. Although provinces were lost and millions were expelled, these calamities did not create a festering sore. Only the scar remains. Several elements combined to purge the poison from a potentially dangerous situation. First, at the end of the war the Germans were in no position to object to their treatment. Defeated and shamed, the atrocities they had committed or had allowed to be committed left them without a shred of international sympathy. Second, the willingness of their fellow countrymen to make room for them and share their meager resources enabled the eastern Germans to create new lives and livelihoods for themselves. Third, the dispossessed people seeking justice for their losses showed remarkable legal and moral restraint.

These three factors, in turn, allowed time to play the role of the great mediator. New generations of Germans refer to the eastern provinces as the homes of their forebears. "My grandparents came from Silesia," conveys a vaguely nostalgic sentiment, reminiscent of a reference to Italy or Ireland made by a third-generation American. Such expressions are abstractions, tied to familial memories. "It would be exciting to visit the old homeland, but I wouldn't want to live there." Why leave a comfortable, familiar world? Young Germans from both east and west know that their standard of living is considerably higher than it would be if they returned to the land of their ancestors.

The cry for justice so eloquently articulated in the past by Germans from the provinces east of the Oder-Neisse rivers softened. It is more difficult now to gather such masses of Silesians as, for example, the 230,000 who assembled in Hannover in 1969. The number of actual participants is dwindling, old age and death taking their toll. But the voice of the *Heimatklaenge* and other such publications is still heard. Their most urgent claims, however, no longer call for restoration of the old boundary. The leadership of the expellee organizations are more likely to seek financial compensation for the properties lost in 1945-46. Their negotiations are directed to the

Central Europe in 1990

German government to enter negotiations with Poland to seek adjustment for assets lost nearly half a century ago. At this point in history their requests have been ignored.

The reunification of Germany on October 3, 1990 was accompanied by solemn declarations to respect the present boundaries. The Polish, Soviet and German heads of state pledged their governments not to seek territorial adjustments. We have no reason to doubt the sincerity of these guarantees.

Winzig remains only as a memory, a memory that will grow fainter with the passage of time. Its story does not have a Hollywood ending. But neither is it a tragedy. Surely justice was badly served when the people were driven out. But Winzigers and the millions of their counterparts refused to pursue a policy of violence and revenge that would do injustice to others. They did not subvert the principles of law to turn right into might. And wisely so! The search for fairness for Winzigers would lead into some dark passages. It would have to probe the concentration camp murders of the elderly Jews unable to escape from Winzig and the 6 million who shared their fate in the German death factories. It would lead up the staircase to Dr. Loele's office and the dead bodies on the floor. It would replay the mysterious death of Mayor Lang, who disappeared from the train as he fled Winzig ahead of the general evacuation in 1945. The thread would become entangled in the suffering of millions, the innocent and the guilty. To what avail?

Truly those who forget the past are condemned to relive it. But what of those who cannot rid themselves of the burdens of their memories? What of those who cannot move beyond their pain? Are they not condemned to a fruitless replay of their grief forever?

Notes

CHAPTER 1. THE GOOD OLD DAYS

1. Albert Scholz, *Silesia Yesterday and Today* (The Hague: Martinus Nyhoff, 1964), pp. 1-15.
2. Ibid., pp. 1-15.
3. Heinrich Schubert, *Chronik der Stadt Winzig* (Breslau: Koenigliche Regierung Preussen, 1859), p. 1.
4. Johannes Spieler, *Vom Wirtschaftlichen Leben Winzigs*, pp. 15-16.
5. Ibid.
6. Walter Wittmann, *Winziger Geschichte: von der Magistratsverfassung und Anderes Mehr*, p. 1.
7. Johannes Spieler, *Vom Wirtschaftlichen Leben Winzigs*, pp. 16-17.
8. Wittmann, *Winziger Geschichte: Von der Magistratsverfassung und Anderes Mehr*, pp. 4-6.

CHAPTER 2. VICTORY BY DEFAULT

1. Wittmann, *Winziger Geschichte*, p. 6.
2. *Der Stahlhelm Muss Sein*, Introduction and Afterword by Hans Hennig Freiherr Grote (Berlin: Stahlhelm Verlag, 1933), pp. 7-11.
3. Johannes Spieler, *Erinnerungen*, pp. 15-16.
4. Alan Bullock, *Hitler, a Study in Tyranny* (New York: Harper and Row, 1962), pp. 199-201.

5. Ibid., p. 201.

6. Walter Wittmann, *Winziger Geschichte*, pp. 1-3.

7. Ibid.

8. Ibid.

9. Ibid.

10. Ibid.

11. Ibid., pp. 4-5.

12. Ibid.

13. Werner Fuchs, *Der Neue Polenspiegel*, a 142-page pamphlet issued in 1930 by the Stahlhelm "proving" that a Polish attack was imminent.

14. *Der Stahlhelm Muss Sein*, p. 49.

15. Ibid., p. 71.

16. Heinrich Hildebrandt and Walter Kettner, eds., *Stahlhelm Handbuch* (Berlin: Stahlhelm Verlag, 1931), p. 49.

17. Bullock, p. 275.

CHAPTER 3. SOMETHING VENTURED, NOTHING GAINED

1. Ernst Roehm, chief of the German SA and Edmund Heine, head of the SA of Silesia were among the victims of the "Night of the Long Knives."

2. Letter to author from Father Willinek, October 17, 1967.

3. Masz, Konrad, *Das Erste Jahr der Regierung Hitler's*, pamphlet no. 52 (Munich: Gottfried Feder Verlag for the NSDAP, 1934), p. 10.

4. Dr. Adolf Dresler and Fritz Maeir-Hartmann, eds., *Dokumente des Dritten Reiches* (Munich: Zentralverlag der NSDAP, 1939), p. 70.

5. *The Nazi Primer: Official Handbook for Schooling the Hitler Youth*, transl. Norwood L. Childs, commentary by William E. Dodd (New York: Harper Brothers, 1934), pp. xvii-xx.

6. Ibid.

7. Karl Friedrich Strum, *Der Geschichtsunterict der Volksschule im Nationalsozialistischen Staate* (Leipzig: Verlag der Duerrscher Buchhandlung, 1933), p. 61.

8. Ibid., p. 12.

9. Dr. Konrad Prentzel, ed., *Neuer Volksschulatlas: Dein*

Land, Dein Volk, Deine Welt (Vielefeld: Velhagen und Kissings Verlag, 1936), p. 10.

10. *Unser Familienbuch* (Berlin: NSDAP Verlag, n.d.), contained instructions for students tracing their ancestry.

11. Nathaniel Micklem, *National Socialism and the Roman Catholic Church* (London: Oxford University Press, 1939), pp. 62-84.

12. William L. Shirer, *The Rise and Fall of the Third Reich* (New York: Fawcett Crest, 1960), pp. 224-232.

13. Johannes Spieler, *Mein Kampf um Recht*, p. 4.

14. Ibid.

15. Ibid., p. 5.

16. Dr. Otto Ganweiler and Dr. Anton Lingg, eds., *Der Partei Richter* (Munich: NSDAP Verlag, 1938), p.15.

17. Johannes Spieler, *Als Nichtparteigenosse vor dem Parteigericht*, p. 1.

18. Ibid., p. 2.

19. Ibid.

20. Ibid., p. 3.

21. Wittmann, *Winziger Geschichte*, pp. 3-4.

22. Ibid., p. 4.

23. Spieler, *Mein Kampf um Recht*, p. 5.

24. Ibid.

25. Ibid.

26. Ibid., p. 6.

27. Ibid.

CHAPTER 4. ANTI-SEMITISM: BLIGHT AND FLIGHT

1. Hermann Grau, Hans Mommsen, Hans Joachim Reichhard, and Ernst Wolf, *The German Resistance to Hitler*, introduction by F. L. Carston (Berkeley: University of California Press, 1970), p. vii.

2. Fritz Max Cahen, *Men against Hitler*, adapted by Wythe Williams (Indianapolis: Bobbs-Merrill, 1939), p. 250.

3. Leon Poliakov, *Harvest of Hate* (Syracuse: Syracuse University Press, 1954), p .10.

4. Helmut Krausnick, Hans Buchheim, Martin Broszart, and Hans-Adolf Jacobsen, *Anatomy of the SS State* (Freiburg: Walter

and Company, 1965), pp. 24-25.

5. Shirer, *The Rise and Fall of the Third Reich*, p. 332.

6. Heymann Steinhardt, *Erinnerungen* (Recollections), pp. 1-2.

7. Poliakov, *Harvest of Hate*, p. 26.

8. Ibid., p. 20.

9. Steinhardt, *Erinnerungen*, pp. 1-4.

10. Krausnick et al., *Anatomy of the SS State*, p. 40.

11. Dr. Jur. Markmann Wagner and Paul Enterlein, eds., *Die Entjudung der Deutschen Wirtschaft* (Berlin: Gersbach und Co., 1938), p. 92.

12. Steinhardt, *Erinnerungen*, p. 6.

13. Ibid., p. 7.

CHAPTER 5. THE DEATH OF WINZIG

1. Theodor Schieder, ed., *Dokumentation der Vertreibung der Deutschen aus Ost-Mitteleuropa*, vol. 1 of *Die Vertreibung der Deutschen Bevoelkerung aus den Gebieten Oestlich der Oder Neisze* (Bonn: Herausgegeben vom Bundesministerium fuer Vertriebene, Fluechtlinge und Kriegsgeschaedigte, 1960), p. 1E.

2. Ibid.

3. H. Royer, ed., *20 Juli 1944* (Bonn: Berto Verlag, 1961), pp. 341-343.

4. Schieder, *Dokumentation der Vertreibung*, p. 8E.

5. Ibid.

6. Ibid., p. 9E.

7. Albert Seaton, *The Russo-German War 1941-1945* (New York: Praeger Publishers, 1970), p. 548.

8. Schieder, *Dokumentation der Vertreibung*, p. 9E.

9. Ibid., pp. 11-13.

10. Juergen Thorwald, *Es Begann an der Weichsel* (Stuttgart: Steingruben Verlag, 1950), pp. 79-80.

11. Seaton, *The Russo-German War*, p. 559.

12. Karl Friedrich Grau, *Schlesisches Inferno* (Stuttgart: Seewald Verlag, 1958), p. 28.

13. *Heimatklaenge*, no. 64.

14. Schieder, *Dokumentation der Vertreibung*, p. 47E.

15. Ibid., pp. 41E-47E.

16. Translation of a *Raemungsbefehl* (evacuation order).

17. *Heimatklaenge*, no. 64.
18. Horses were evaluated; those fit to work were commandeered by the army.
19. *Heimatklaenge*, no. 83.
20. Letter from Hugo Kliem to Heymann Steinhardt.
21. Ibid.
22. Schieder, *Dokumentation der Verteibung*, p. 62E.
23. Letter from Alois Stiller to Heymann Steinhardt.
24. *Heimatklaenge*, no. 20.
25. Schieder, *Dokumentation der Vertreibung*, p. 56E.
26. *Heimatklaenge*, no. 53.
27. *Heimatklaenge*, no. 56.

CHAPTER 6. THE ODER-NEISSE LINE: FOCUS OF CONFLICTING CLAIMS

1. Vaclav L. Benes and Norman J. G. Pounds, *Nations of the Modern World: Poland* (New York: Praeger Publishers, 1970), p. 2.
2. Clifford Barnett, *Poland* (New Haven: Hraf Press, 1958), p. 21.
3. Winston Churchill, *The Second Word War: Triumph and Tragedy* (Boston: Houghton Miffling, 1953), p. 366.
4. Ibid., p. 374.
5. Ibid.
6. Henry Steele Commanger, ed., *Documents of American History* (New York: Appelton-Century-Crofts, 1957), p. 491.
7. *Das Potsdamer Abkommen und Andere Dokumente*, (Berlin: Kongress Verlag, 1950), p. 4.
8. *W.V. Leahy*, "I Was There," in Gotthold Rhode and Wofgang Wagner, eds., *The Genesis of the Oder-Neisse Line: Sources and Documents* (Stuttgart: Brentano Verlag, 1954), p. 447.
9. A. Bliss Lane, "I Saw Poland Betrayed," in Rhode and Wagner, *The Genesis of the Oder-Neisse Line*, p. 218.
10. *Das Potsdamer Abkommen und Andere Dokumente*, p. 188.
11. Harry S. Truman, *Public Papers of the President* (Washington, DC: U.S. Government Printing Office, 1961), pp. 191-192.

12. "Text of the the Pact between Poland and West Germany," *New York Times*, November 21, 1970, p. 11.

13. *The Week in Germany*, November 17, 1989, p. 2.

14. Ibid.

15. *Polish Western Affairs*, p. 7.

16. Ibid.

17. Manfred Lachs, *The Polish German Frontier, Law, Life and Logic of History* (Warsaw: PWN-Polish Scientific Publishers, 1964), p. 21.

18. *Polish Western Affairs*, p. 74.

19. Ibid.

20. *The Week in Germany*, November 17, 1989, p. 2.

21. Schieder, *Dokumentation der Vertreibung*, p. 4E.

22. *Heimatklaenge: Sonderausgabe* (special anniversary edition), p. 3.

23. *Heimatklaenge*, no. 35.

24. Ibid., no. 34.

25. Ibid.

26. Ibid.

Annotated Bibliography

PRIMARY SOURCES

Published

Asner, Walter, ed. *Das Dritte Reich in Dokumentum*. Frankfurt am Main: Europaeischer Verlag, 1957.

Beyer, Rudolf, ed. *Hitlergesetze XIII: Die Nuernberger Gesetze*. Leipzig: Philipp Reclam, 1936. Compilation of a series of laws generally known as the Nueremberg Laws.

Brandt, Alfred Ingmar, ed. *Gebt mir Vier Jahre Zeit, Dokumenten zum Ersten Vierjahres Plan des Fuehrers*. Munich: Zentralverlag der NSDAP, 1937. Introduction by Dr. Joseph Goebbels. A list of the laws promulgated during the first four years of Hitler's dictatorship.

Churchill, Winston. *The Second World War: Triumph and Tragedy*. Boston: Houghton Mifflin, 1953.

Commanger, Henry Steele, ed. *Documents of American History*. New York: Appelton-Century-Crofts, 1957.

Dierke. *Schulatlas fuer Hoehere Lehranstalten*. Berlin: Verlag von Georg Westerman, 1936. Nazi version of world geography. Dr. Adolf Dresler and Fritz Maier-Hartmann, eds. *Dokumente des Dritten Reiches*. Munich: Zentralverlag der NSDAP, 1939.

Freisler, dr. Roland. *Nationalsozialistiches Recht und Rechtsdenker*. Berlin: Industrie Verlag Spaeth und Linde, 1938.

Delineation of Nazi concept of justice: the highest function of the law is service to the state.

Ganweiler, Dr. Otto, and Dr. Anton Lingg, eds. *Der Partei Richter*. Berlin: Verlag der NSDAP, 1938. Journal published for members of the Nazi party's own judicial system.

Gau und Kreisverzeichnis der NSDAP. Berlin: Verlag der NSDAP, n.d. Officially issued statistics, charts, and tables on membership in the Nazi party.

Gewerklichen Vertriebenen und Fluechtlingsbetriebe, Die. Bad Godesberg: Lasten Ausgleich Bank, 1955. Report from the West German bank responsible for aid to expellees from the eastern territories concerning assistance to and integration of this population into West German economic life.

Heimatklaenge, edited by Father Joseph Willinek. Meschede, Germany: N.P., 1948. Newsletters published three or four times a year written by and for former residents of Winzig. Contain memoirs of pre-Nazi life, the Hitlerian era, the war years, and the expulsion as well as news since the resettlement in the West.

Hildebrandt, Heinrich and Walter Kettner, eds. *Stahlhelm Handbuch*. Berlin: Stahlhelm Verlag, 1931. Handbook for veterans that expresses the ultrarightist policies of this supposedly suprapolitical organization.

Kappas, Dr. Johannes, ed. *Die Tragoedie Schlesiens 1945/46 in Dokumenten*. Munich: Christ Unterwegs Verlag, 1951.

Langer, Erwin. *Deutscher Frontkaempferglaube*. Breslau: Ferdian Hirt, 1935. Pamphlet published by the Stahlhelm organization, with a foreword by the censor of the Nazi party. Glorifies the military and rightwing politics.

Masz, Konrad. *Das Erste Jahr der Regierung Hitler's*, pamphlet 52. Berlin: Gottfried Feder Verlag for the NSDAP, 1934. Propaganda tract that extols the elimination of democratic institutions during Hitler's first year.

Mathias, Erich, and Rudolf Morsey. *Das Ende der Parteien*. Duesseldorf: Broste Verlag, 1960. Statistics and analysis of the 1933 election results.

Nazi Primer: The Official Handbook for Schooling the Hitler Youth. Translated by Norwood L. Childs. New York: Harper Brothers, 1938. Introduction and commentary by former U.S. ambassador to Germany William E. Dowd.

New York Times, May 31, 1970. "Text of the Pact between Poland and West Germany." November 21, 1970. "A New Poland Rises on Oder."

Polish Western Affairs. Poznan: Institute for Polish Western Affairs, vol. 2, no. 1, 1961; vol. 6, no. 2, 1965. Pamphlets containing articles of sociological and historical interest relating to western Poland.

Potsdamer Abkommen und Andere Dokumente, Das. Berlin: Kongress Verlag, 1950. Published in East Germany; documents are accompanied by anti-Western editorial comments.

Prentzel, Dr. Konrad, ed. *Neuer Schulatlas: Dein Land, Dein Volk, Deine Welt*. Vielefeld: Velhagen und Kissings Verlag, 1936. Atlas used in German schools during Nazi years, full of propaganda and distortions.

Remak, Joachim, ed. *The Nazi Years: A Documentary History*. Englewood Cliffs, NJ: Prentice Hall, 1969.

Rhode, Gotthold and Wolfgang Wagner, eds. *The Genesis of the Oder-Neisse Line: Sources and Documents*. Stuttgart: Brentano Verlag, 1954.

Royer, H., ed. *20 July 1944*. Bonn: Berto Verlag, 1961. A documentary account of the failed attempt on Hitler's life and its consequences.

Schieder, Theodor, ed. *Dokumentation der Vertreibung der Deutschen aus Ost-Mitteleuropa*, 3 vols. Bonn: Herausgegeben vom Bundesministerium fuer Vertriebene, Fluechtlinge, und Kriegsgeschaedigte, 1960. Three volumes of eyewitness documentation on the expulsion of the German population from the territories east of the Oder-Neisse Line. Dr. Schieder is the leading historian on the expulsion.

Schirach, Baldur von. *Die Hitlerjugend, Idee und Gestalt*. Berlin: Zeitgeschichte Verlag, 1934. Nazi youth leader explains aims and organization of Hitler Youth movement.

Schubert, Heinrich. *Chronik der Stadt Winzig*. Breslau: Koenigliche Regierung Preussen, 1859. Author was town's pharmacist; description of history and life in Winzig is episodic rather than scholarly.

Stahlhelm Muss Sein, Der. Introduction and afterword by Hans Henning Freiherr Grote. Berlin: Stahlhelm Verlag, 1933. A pathetic effort of the Stahlhelm to stave off its absorption by the NSDAP by pointing up the similarities of the two organizations.

Sturm, Karl Friedrich. *Der Geschichtsunterricht der Volksschule im Nationalsozialistichen Staate.* Leipzig: Verlag der Duerrscher Buchhandlung, 1933. An official of the Nazi Education Ministry explains that the teaching of history must conform to racial theories.

Truman, Harry S. *Public Papers of the President.* Washington, DC: U.S. Government Printing Office, 1961.

Unser Familienbuch. Berlin: NSDAP Verlag, n.d. A pamphlet giving instructions for the tracing of genealogical background required by all German students during the Nazi era.

Wagner, Dr. Jur. Markmann, and Paul Enterlein, eds. *Die Entjudung der Deutschen Wirtschaft.* Berlin: Gersbach und Co, 1938. A compilation of the laws which drove the Jews from the German economy during the Nazi era.

Week in Germany, The. November 17, 1989. "Kohl Terms Poland Visit a Success." New York: German Information Center.

Unpublished

Botwinick, Rita S. "The Story of Winzig 1933-1945: Silesian Fate in Microcosm". Ph.D. diss. St. John's University, New York, 1973. The material listed below is deposited at St John's in connection with the dissertation.

Kliem, Hugo. Letters to Heymann Steinhardt, 1945 to 1972.

Spieler, Johannes. Erinnerungen (Recollections) 1945-1955, titled:
Vom Wirkschaflichen Leben Winzigs;
Meine Kampf um Recht;
Als NichtParteigenosse vor dem Parteigericht.

Steinhardt, Heymann. *Erinnerungen* (Recollections) 1950-1970.

Stiller, Alois. Letters to Heymann Steinhardt 1945-1958.

Willinek, Fr. Joseph. Letters to Rita Botwinick 1945-1972.

Wittmann, Walter. *Winziger Geschichte: Von der Magistratsverfassung und Anderes Mehr,* 1945-1955

SECONDARY SOURCES

Alfen, General Major Hans von. *Der Kampf um Schlesien.* Munich: Graefe und Unzer Verlag, 1961. Silesian war history by a participating general.

Allen, William Sheridan. *The Nazi Seizure of Power: The Experience of a Single German Town, 1930-1935.* Chicago: Quadrangle Books, 1965.

Barnett, Clifford. *Poland.* New Haven: Hraf Press, 1958.

Brandt, Willy. *A Peace Policy for Europe.* Translated by Joel Carmichael. New York: Holt, Rinehart and Winston, 1969.

Bullock, Alan. *Hitler: A Study in Tyranny.* New York: Harper and Row, 1962.

Cahen, Fritz Max. *Men Against Hitler.* Adapted by Wythe Williams. Indianapolis: Bobbs-Merrill Company, 1939.

Dulles, Allen Welch. *Germany's Underground.* New York: MacMillan 1947.

Grau, Karl Friedrich. *Schlesiches Inferno.* Stuttgart: Seewald Verlag, 1958.

Graul, Hermann, Hans Mommsen, Hans Joachim Reichard, and Ernst Wolf. *The German Resistance to Hitler.* Introduction by F. L. Carston. Berkeley: University of California Press, 1970.

Gruchman, Bodhan, Alfons Klafkowski, Juliuz Kolopinski, Kasimiriez Piwarski, Edward Serwanski, Stanislawa Zahchowska, and Jansz Ziolkowski. *Polish Western Territories.* Posnan: Instytut Zachodni, 1939.

Hilbert, Raul. *The Destruction of the European Jews.* Chicago: Quadrangle Books, 1959.

Hoehne, Heinz. *The Order of the Death Head.* New York: Ballantine Books, 1971.

Juergen, Thorwald. *Es Began an der Weichsel.* Stuttgart: Steingruben Verlag, 1950.

Kapps, Dr. Johannes. *The Tragedy of Silesia.* Translated by Gladys H. Hartinger. Munich: Christ Unterwegs Verlag, 1952.

Krausnick, Helmut, Hans Buchheim, Martin Broszart, and Hans-Adolf Jacobsen. *Anatomy of SS State.* Freiburg: Walter and Company, 1965.

Lachs, Manfred, *The Polish-German Frontier, Law, Life and Logic of History.* Warsaw: PWN-Polish Scientific Publishers, 1964.

Mickelm, Nathaniel. *National Socialism and the Roman Catholic Church*. London: Oxford University Press, 1939.

Poliakov, Leon, *Harvest of Hate*. Syracuse: Syracuse University Press, 1954.

Scholz, Albert. *Silesia Yesterday and Today*. The Hague: Martinus Nijhoff, 1964.

Shirer, William, L. *The Rise and Fall of the Third Reich*. New York: Fawcett Crest, 1960.

Seaton, Albert. *The Russo-German War 1041-1945*. New York: Praeger Publishers, 1970.

Wilpert, F. *The Oder-Neisse Problem*. Bonn: Edition Atlantic Forum, 1964.

Index

Allied Control Council,
123
Allies, 6, 92, 102, 114,
115; air raids, 88, 89;
invasion of Germany, 90
All-Silesian Assembly, 130
Arnholtz family, 66, 67,
73, 79
Aryan, 43, 44
"Aryanization" of property,
82
Anti-Nazi activities, 3, 29,
74, 89-90
Anti-Semitism, 16, 65-85;
Krystallnacht, 76-83;
legislation, 68-72, 76,
83; in Winzig, 65, 66-
68. See also Jews
Auschwitz, 66
Atlee, Clement, 117
Aust, Walter, 21, 24
Axis Powers, 102

Baenkelsaenger, 17
Berlin, 20, 49-50, 73, 78,
83-85
Berns, Max, 73, 78, 84

Big Three, 112, 113, 115-
20
Blackshirts. See SS
Boerner, Reverend, 46,
109-10
Boycott, 70, 71
Breslau (Wroclaw),
1, 10, 20, 57, 58, 71,
72, 89; battle for, 93,
107; Krystallnacht,
79-82; Patenstadt, 127;
Polish city, 121
Brownshirts. See SA
Bruening, Heinrich, 25, 29
Buchenwald concentration
camp, 78
Bug River, 113, 121
Brandt, Willy, 120
British Zone of Occupa-
tion, 110, 124

Cahen, Fritz Max, 64
Carston, F. L., 64
Catholic Center party, 19,
20, 25
Celts, 10
Center party. See Catholic

Center party
Churchill, Winston, 112-7
Communist party, 25, 28,
    31, 36, 64
Concordat of 1933, 45
Curzon Line, 113, 114,
    116
Czechoslovakia, 95, 99,
    105, 118

Dachau concentration
    camp, 73, 78
Daunert, Schulrat, 55-58
Dick, Englebert, 130-31
Dresden, 5
Duesterberg, Theodor, 27,
    28, 36

East Germany (German
Democratic Republic), 113,
    120, 127
East Prussia, 95, 110, 121
Ebert, Friedrich, 23
Emigration, 68, 85
Enabling Act, 31
Evacuation of German
    civilians: before Red
    Army 123; from Poland,
    90, 93-94; from Silesia,
    93-95; from Winzig,
    95-105; return of
    evacuees, 105-7
Evacuation Order, 95-96;
    refusal to obey, 98, 102
Expulsion of German ci-
    vilians, 4, 5; attempts to
    regain lost territories,
    131-4; from east of
    Oder-Neisse Line, 124;
    from Winzig, 110, 111,

123, 124

Familienbuch, 44
"Final Solution," 5, 72
France, 85, 115
Frederick the Great, 10,
    18, 115
Fromm, Erich, 62

Gauleiter, 4, 5, 32, 90-92
Genocide, 65, 69, 72
German Democratic party,
    19, 20
German Democratic Re-
    public. See East Ger-
    many
German Federal Republic.
    See West Germany
German Jews, 66-69, 70,
    75, 76; Nuremberg
    Laws, 72, 73. See also
    Anti-Semitism
German-National People's
    party, 19
German People's party, 19
German Republican party,
    121
Germany, pre-Nazi, 2, 3.
    See also Weimar Repub-
    lic
Germany, Third Reich, 3,
    4, 53; Agrarian Laws,
    42; attack on
    Poland, 86; attack on
    Soviet Union, 5, 116;
    education, 42-44, 71;
    Jews in, see Anti-
    Semitism, German Jews;
    life 1933-39, 41, 61;
    political life, 30, 31, 35;

religion, 45, 46; since
World War II, 5,
121, 124, 133, 134;
unemployment, 23, 41;
zones of occupation,
115; Germany, reunified,
132
Gestapo, 61, 74, 77, 89
Goebbels, Joseph (Propa-
ganda Ministry), 4, 27,
53, 89; anti-Jewish pro-
paganda, 69, 77;
anti-Polish propaganda,
87; as Plenipotentiary for
the Winning of the War,
90, 91
Goering Hermann, 33, 77
Grenzschutz, 33, 34
Grote, Freiherr Hans Hen-
nig von, 36
Grynspan, Herschel, 76, 77
Guhrau, 58
Gute Stube, 15
Gymnasium, 15, 73

Hanke, Gauleiter Karl, 94
Hedwig, Ste., 10
Heimatklaenge, 96,
125-27, 130
Henry I (Piast), 10
Hildebrandt, affair, 47-53
Himmler, Heinrich, 77
Hindenburg, General Paul
von, 25, 27-30
Hitler, Adolph, 1-4, 28,
36, 41, 43, 61; assassi-
nation attempt, 89-91;
elections, 25, 27, 28, 29,
30; Hildebrandt
audience, 49-50;

Jews, 62, 68, 75;
"Night of the Long
Knives," 40; sources of
support, 26, 61, 62, 64;
World War II, 90
Hitler-Stalin Non-aggres-
sion Pact, 114
Hitler Youth, 43, 44, 64,
70; handbook, 43
Holland (Netherlands), 74
Holocaust, 5, 66, 67, 73,
111, 133. *See also*
"Final Solution"

Ilyrians, 10

Jahrmarkt, 17, 18
Jews, 4, 5, 42-44, 62, 83;
identification, 65; isola-
tion, 65, 71
Juerke, Max, 31-32
July 20 attempt on Hitler's
life, 89-90
Junker class, 26

Kabinetsorder, 19
Kinderfest, 18, 19, 46, 47,
56, 73
Kliem, Ernst, 13, 14, 40
Kliem, Hugo, 3, 13, 42,
65, 74, 122; during boy-
cott, 70-71; during
Soviet invasion, 102-5
political views, 28, 75-
76, 82, 85
Koch, *Rittergutsbesitzer*,
75
Kohl, Chancellor Helmut,
120, 122
Konev, General Ivan, 92,

94, 102
Krause, Mayor, 20, 21, 23
Krystallnacht, 69, 73, 76;
   causes, 76-77; events,
   77-82; Heymann
   Steinhardt's escape,
   79-83; results, 82-83

Lachs, Manfred, 123
Lang, Mayor Joachim,
   31-35, 39; as Mayor, 40,
   45, 47; in Hildebrandt
   Affair, 47-52; in
   Spieler's struggle, 54-59;
   and Steinhardt family,
   84-85; Winzig's last
   days, 97
League of Expellees, 127
Lenin, V.I., 114
Loele, Dr., 67, 76, 98-99,
   101-3, 133
Lustwald, 18, 19, 23, 46
Lutheran (Evangelical)
   church, 7, 46, 108

Mai, Georg, 42, 43, 54-59,
   71
Maltsch, 58
Matschke, Elfriede, 96,
   99-101
Mazowieke, Tadeusze, 120
Mein Kampf, 71
Meschede, 124, 128, 130
Mischling, 72, 73
Molotov, Vyacheslav, 115
Moses family, 66;
   Anna, 63, 73, 79, 82;
   Jakob, 73; Josef, 73;
   Margot, 42-46, 47, 73;
   Ruth (Berns), 73, 78, 82

Nacht und Nebel, 61, 74
Netherlands, 72
Niemueller, Pastor Martin,
   46
"Night of the Long
   Knives," 40. See also
   SA
Nitschke, Theodor, 29
NSDAP (Nazi party), 1-4,
   34, 62-65; elections,
   27-30; membership,
   41, 44, 63-64; party
   court, 4, 50-53
Nuremberg Laws, 72, 73
Nuremberg War Crimes
   Tribunal, 65, 111

Oder-Neisse Line, 3-6,
   106, 111-30; cession to
   Poland, 106, 119, 120;
   delineation, 115, 117-9;
   in re expellees' politics,
   130, 133; origin, 112,
   115
Oder River, 1, 11; in
   World War II, 92,
   97, 99, 102
Operation Swallow, 124

Pantken, 29
Papen, Franz von, 29, 30
Patenstadt, 127-30
Piast Dynasty, 10, 14, 113
Poland (Polish People's
   Republic), 1, 3, 4, 10,
   35, 44, 66; boundary
   established, 6, 114, 115;
   expulsion of Germans,
   5, 124, 125; in World

War II, 84, 87, 115;
legitimization of boun-
dary, 119-22; Ministry
for Recovered Ter-
ritories, 121;
Polish sovereignty of
Oder-Neisse territories,
5, 6, 109, 115-7; post
World War II, 120, 121,
123, 127; prisoners of
war, 88; remaining eth-
nic Germans 123; trea-
ties on Oder-Neisse
Line, 120; western ex-
pansion, 112, 113-24;
Winzig occupation au-
thorities, 108-11
Polish-British Commission,
124
Polish Provisional Government, 118, 119
Polish Western Affairs,
122
Politburo, 5
Pomerania, 95, 110, 121,
127, 129
Potsdam Conference, 112,
117, 119-2
Prussia, 1, 10, 127

Rassenkunde, 43
Rassenschande, 85
Rath, Ernst vom, 76, 77,
82
Red Army (Soviet Army),
4, 5, 6, 89, 91-95, 107;
flight from, 94, 102; in
Winzig, 102-7
Reichsbanner Schwarz-
Rot-Gold, 25, 28, 35,

55 Reichstag, 26, 29,
30, 31
Ridder, Justice von, 51,
52, 53, 54
Riga, Treaty of, 114
Rittergutsbesitzer, 13
Rommel, General Erwin,
89
Roosevelt, Franklin
Delano, 112, 114, 117
Ruchatz, Schulrat Dr., 57-
58
Ruhr, 27
Rust, Dr. Bernard, 43, 58

SA (Schutzabteilung) 27,
29, 36, 40, 70-72; dur-
ing Krystallnacht, 77,
78; in Winzig, 32-35,
54, 70, 75-80
Saar, 45
Sauerland, 122, 127
Schandsaeule, 53
Schaube, Amtsgerichtsrat,
31-35, 53, 84-85; as
town administrator,
40, 45, 47; in "Poem of
the Pump," 40
Schleicher, General Kurt
von, 30
Schwerdtner, Karl, 107,
109
Seldte, Franz, 25, 36
Silesia, 1, 9, 10, 25, 35;
cession to Poland, 110,
113, 118; dialect, 10;
economy, 13; exodus
from, 94, 95, 99, 111;
history, 10, 14, 18, 121;
"Night of the Long

Knives," 40; post-World
    War II, 121, 127,
    131; during World War
    II, 88, 89, 91, 98
Sillingi, 10
Slave laborers, 88, 107,
    125
Slavs, 10
Social Democratic party,
    19, 20, 31
Soviet Union, 3, 4, 5, 6,
    120, 130; cession from
    Poland, 113-6; cession to
    Poland, 5, 114-8;
    counter-offensive, see
    Red Army; Curzon Line,
    113, 114, 116; zone of
    occupation, 118, 119,
    123
Spieler, Rektor Johannes,
    3, 4, 12, 18, 63, 65; in
    Battle for Honor and
    Right, 54-59; in
    Hildebrandt affair, 51-52;
    and Kinderfest, 46, 47;
    political estimates, 19;
    after World War II, 125
SS (Schutzstaffel) 40,
    77-81, 88, 89, 91
Staemplers, 24, 42
Stahlhelm, 19, 25-28,
    33-36, 53, 54
Stalin, Joseph, 112, 113-8
Steinau, 11, 34, 35, 42,
    78; during World War
    II, 92-93, 102
Steinhardt family, 5, 28,
    66, 74; emigration, 83-
    85; Heymann, 42, 63,
    66, 78-85; Josef, 74;

Rita, 42, 47, 71-72, 84;
    Rosa, 74, 78; Siegfried,
    56, 71, 83; Walter, 74
Stiller, Alois, 104-7
Stettin, 1, 115
System, Das, 26

Tehran Conference, 112,
    114
Third Reich. See also Ger-
    many, 44, 53, 54, 63,
    64
Truman, Harry, 112, 117
Typhoid, 108

Union of Silesians, 126,
    130
United Nations, 6, 115,
    120
United States, 66, 73-76,
    117; Department of
    State, 83; National
    Origins Act, 83; U.S.
    Consul (Berlin), 83-85;
    zone of occupation, 123

Vandals, 10
Versailles, Treaty, 23, 27,
    35, 65, 66, 113
Vistula River, 91
Volkssturm, 91, 96, 97,
    125

Warsaw Treaty, 120
Wartheland, Gau, 92
Weimar Republic, 19, 23,
    5-31
Western Allies, 6, 117,
    119
West Germany, (German

Federal Republic), 66, 120, 122, 123
Westphalia, 124, 125
West Prussia, 95, 110, 128
Wilhelm I, 19
Wilhelm II, 20, 23, 26
Willinek, Ernst, 41
Willinek, Father Joseph, 41, 45, 63, 93-94; evacuation of Winzig, 96-99; founder of *Heimatklaenge*, 125-27; Patenstadt arrangements, 128-130
Winsco, 1, 110, 122
Winzig, 1, 3, 4, 10; architecture, 14; boycott, 70, 71; Catholics, 45; economics, 2, 11-13, 24; education, 15, 16, 42-44; elections, 28, 29; evacuation, 6, 96-105; final exodus, 109-14; geography, 9, 10; Hildebrandt affair, 47-53; history, 5, 9, 11; Jewish population, 4, 16, 41, 53, 65-83; Krystallnacht, 78-82; pre World War II, 9-21, 41, 55, 65; Nazi party, 31-35; Patenstadt arrangements, 127-131; police force, 17; politics, 20-23, 25, 29; Protestants, 15; Polish administration, 3, 108-11; political life, 12, 19-21, 27, 31-35, 47-59, 63-65; religion, 15, 16, 17, 41, 45; returnees of

1945, 108, 123; SA, 32, 33, 70; social life, 14, 17, 46; Soviet invasion, 3, 4, 5, 29, 101-7; Soviet occupation, 102-8; Spieler's struggle, 54-59; town council, 32-33; Weimar years, 24; World War II years, 87-94
Wittmann, Walter, 20, 32, 34, 40
Wohlau, 10, 11, 18, 21, 48, 51, 79, 127
World War I, 2, 19, 21, 25, 26, 33, 35, 88
World War II, 84, 87. *See also* Allies; Evacuation of German civilians; Grenzschutz; Hitler; Soviet Union; Tehran Conference
Yalta Conference
Wroclaw. *See* Breslau

Yalta Conference, 112, 115-17

Zhukov, General Georgi, 92
Zones of Allied occupation, 115, 123, 124, 127

About the Author

RITA S. BOTWINICK is on the faculty of Florida Atlantic University, where she teaches European history and the Holocaust. Dr. Botwinick, who holds a Ph.D. from St. John's University, was born in Winzig, Germany and lived there until the age of sixteen, when she and some members of her family escaped to the United States. After World War II contacts with former Winzigers were renewed. As a result, she was able to personally document the events that occurred in Winzig in the 1940s.